Taken By Surprise

Cutting-Edge Collaborations between
Designers, Artists, and Brands

gestalten

Contents

5.5 Designers, ...,staat, Saâdane Afif, Amigos del Museo de Arte Popular, Frank Anselmo, Ron Arad, Omer Arbel, Jorge Julián Aristizábal, ART+COM, avaf, Francois Azambourg, Maarten Baas, Marian Bantjes, Bates 141, Yves Béhar, BLANQ, Bompas & Parr, Byggstudio, Campanas Brothers, Scott Campbell, Rafael de Cárdenas, Jean-Charles de Castelbajac, Daniel Chadwick, Hussein Chalayan, David&Goliath, DDB, Tom Dixon, Dorten, Drake, Dror, Olafur Eliasson, ENIA-Architectes , Fabrica, Geoff McFetridge, Fiona Leahy Design, Flea, Foam, Formavision, Front, Thierry Gaugain, Jean Paul Gaultier, John Gerrard, Liam Gillick, Pierre Gonalons, Martí Guixé, Hans Tan Studio, www.hanstan.net, Jaime Hayon I Hayon Studio BCN, Heimat Berlin, Damien Hirst, House Industries, Ideas Generation, Sarah Illenberger, Ilovedust, InkValley, J. MAYER H. Architects, Gerry Judah, Anish Kapoor, Jeff Koons, KRADS, Krink, Karl Lagerfeld, Arnaud Lapierre, Tim Lee, Amanda Lepore, lg2, LOVE, David Lynch, MAD Architects, Philippe Malouin, Stefan Marx, Mash, Jonathan Meese, Alessandro Mendini, Sebastian Menschhorn, Issey Miyake, Jonathan Monk, Matt W. Moore, Sarah Morris, Raphaël Navot, Sebastian Neeb, Nendo, Marc Newson, Willem Nieland, Fabio Novembre, Alexander Olch, Owen & Stork, PandaPanther, Satyendra Pakhalé, Antoine Peters, Porfiristudio, Tom Price, Tobias Rehberger, Terry Richardson, Jerome C. Rousseau, Rolf Sachs, Tom Sachs, Stefan Sagmeister, Ralf Schmerberg, Julian Schnabel, Serviceplan, Cindy Sherman, Jane Simpson, David Shrigley, Sociedad Anónima, Tim Van Steenbergen, Elisa Strozyk, Studio Job, Peter Sutherland, Yuri Suzuki, Trigger Happy Productions, Ogura Tansu Ten, THEY, UbachsWisbrun/JWT, Viktor & Rolf, Moritz Waldemeyer, Gerry Wedd, The Why Factory, Pharrell Williams, Robert Wilson, Erwin Wurm, Li Xiaofeng.

Preface

Taken By Surprise

1

Back in the day, an epic battle raged on MTV: Pepsi vs. Coca Cola for the global soft drink empire. For all practical purposes, Michael Jackson struck a $5 million deal with PepsiCo that would shatter the record for celebrity endorsements and set the bar for every integrated marketing campaign to follow. Both Jackson and his empire would demise slowly, and the reality of brand marketing catch up all the quicker.

It wasn't long before the soft drink duel turned into a pub brawl. Dog-eat-dog, the "Pepsi vs. Coke" battle of the 1980s became "Pepsi vs. Coke vs. Dr Pepper vs. RC Cola vs. Virgin Cola vs. Red Bull Cola vs. Ubuntu Cola vs. Mecca Cola vs. Afri-Cola vs. Dr Skipper vs. Dr Perky vs. Dr Thunder," and on and on. Add the world domination fantasies coming from an Austrian energy drink that tastes like gummy bears and promises teenagers to give them wings, inciting them to jump off cliffs in their underwear, and you have all the ingredients for collective marketing entropy.

"You are what you buy" remains the marketing axiom, but it appears to be overshadowed by the attendant and increasingly agonizing question of "what to buy." Today, The Coca Cola Company pays rap star 50 Cent over $100 million to "design" a special edition of its Vitamin Water and sets up "Happiness Vending Machines" that dispense not only

1 | P. 242
Moritz Waldemeyer
× Hussein Chalayan
Readings (Laser Dresses), 2007

Coke cans but free goodies (that is to say: "happiness"). Evian has its water bottles designed by Issey Miyake, Jean Paul Gaultier, and Christian Lacroix. Absolut Vodka hosts art exhibitions and produces films with Spike Jonze, and Smirnoff parties with Madonna in its Nightlife Exchange Project in search for the "Most Original Nightlife in the Universe." Branding has distorted the logic of value and the world seems to have accepted it with overwrought acquiescence.

Beyond the grand pastiche lies the craving for identity, the necessity to keep up and prevail against an ever-growing crowd of competitors. The technological developments of the last decades have greatly altered the way we work, consume, and communicate. Competition is global, fierce, and growing. A disparate mass of brand messages is hurled at us daily—whether we can't get enough of it or we feel sick of it all. We are all friends in a global community called the internet, which brings about a horrendous mass of information—a large part of which just flashes by.

Both brands and artists need to be increasingly creative in order to reach their audiences. Triggered by harsh market conditions, they must keep changing and progressing with new modes of communication. To increase the rate of transmission and win (back) the consumer's attention, brand messages are set afloat to spread and multiply. The resulting flows of information are as vital to the creation of modern myths as they are to modern marketing. Branding and living merge into a common stream. Consumers become mediators for brand messages, which are a muddle of opinions, remarks, snapshots, and stories.

Nestled in that bundle of raw ideas and un-digested information, a new era of new work is being prepared: artistic and elastic statements that, without a doubt, are shifting between all kinds of disciplines and dimensions. Their independent spirit departs from the mainstream and merges "savoir-vendre" with "savoir-faire" to bring along more novelties, more unconventional approaches, and more sheer energy than the world of marketing has witnessed at any time before.

The variety of brand communication is reflected in this publication. Taken by Surprise investigates the status of branding in contemporary consumer culture. Branding can be a mode that communicates, informs, feeds, supports, describes, backs up, interprets, comments, and reflects upon contemporary creative production. Branding is the core practice of a number of artists, architects, and designers, and is a practice that exists as part of and in constant interchange with visual culture.

Readers will encounter tattooed car tires, interactive computer-controlled chandeliers, and fashion collections animated by the latest lighting technology. They will witness window installations that make books magically come to life, origami sheets that pop up into champagne coolers, or be surprised by the unimagined ambitions of pop stars and filmmakers designing chairs. Roles shift, connect, and merge to the extent that there seems to be only one universal yet malleable discipline that aspires to higher things, moving constantly between dimensions and possibly trying to define a new one.

Much more than a product's physical characteristics, a brand is a concept of astonishing complexity. In order to personalize abstractions, brands calibrate signature elements as a targeted attempt to develop and foster a brand personality. The challenge lies in closing the gap between the visually-identifiable brand identity and the intangible thing it stands for.

Exploring and challenging creative margins of corporate communication and signature calibration, Taken by Surprise sets out to explore branding as a state of mind, a personality, that can certainly be anything from enthusiastic to loveable to neurotic. It looks into works of art, design, advertising, and everything in between, and showcases projects that are linked by an underlying notion of creative

2 | PP. 90–91
Tom Dixon for
Veuve Clicquot
Comet Lamp, 2009

"Pepsi vs. Coke vs. Dr Pepper vs. RC Cola vs. Virgin Cola vs. Red Bull Cola vs. Ubuntu Cola vs. Mecca Cola vs. Afri-Cola vs. Dr Skipper vs. Dr Perky vs. Dr Thunder, and on and on."

1

self-expression. Brand communication, this book argues and exemplifies, has many forms.

Portrayed here are cases of creative line extension, limited edition products, exclusive events, and corporate installations—collaborations, both between one brand and another, and between brands, contemporary artists, and cutting edge designers. These examples show how such projects can benefit both parties, and also how essential it is for a brand to choose the right partner to work with: one that relates to its own values, products, and heritage in one way or another. BMW chose Olafur Eliasson[1], harnessing the contextual, scientifically-minded approach of the Danish artist to create a halo car that actually shines due to mono-frequency lighting. The car was the impressive outcome of an extensive research project investigating the hydrogen-powered BMW H2R. Julian Schnabel collaborated with Maybach, both on a unique art car installation, and with the Wilhelm & Karl Maybach Foundation's mentoring program, which Schnabel assists in order to identify and support young

highly-talented individuals. French clothing and accessory retailer Colette teamed up with the New York-based photographer Terry Richardson, an alliance of a radical pioneering spirit that departs from fashion's pop culture avant-garde. Presenting a collection of various accessory products, the collaborative exhibition toured globally, following its Paris launch on the boutique's own premises.

While many partnerships seem to suggest themselves, the connection or spriritual kinship is not always all that obvious. Some combinations provoke, at least at first glance, a certain amount of wonder. One may not, for example, assume that a traditional glassware manufacturer would turn to one of the most celebrated players of the contemporary graphic design scene to have the concept of a centuries-old project revived. Yet J. & L. Lobmeyr did this, and Stefan Sagmeister's reinterpretation of Adolf Loos's resurrected design idea for a glassware edition unmistakably shows that the brand did well in choosing him. More surprising, if not bewildering, is that the technological features and visual characteristics of a vacuum cleaner could be of any use for a high fashion brand—but Issey Miyake and Dyson created a turbulent fashion line and catwalk show that proved the opposite.

Instead of focusing on the product, some endeavors intend to stage and spotlight the creative process. For example, at the Schinkel Pavillon in Berlin, traditional German porcelain manufactory Nymphenburg presented a one-of-a-kind performance. To illustrate the multidisciplinary substance of the Fairytale Recordings, a collection of vases developed in collaboration with with French performance artist Saâdane Afif and Zurich-based gallery RaebervonStenglin, Nymphenburg invited opera singer and actress Katharina Schrade to relate the poses that the design of the vases is based on. At a temporary space at Design Miami, designer Elisa Strozyk and artist Sebastian Neeb collaborated with Fendi. Using the luxury accessory brand's discarded leather materials, the creative newcomers transformed traditional Italian furniture into objects of leather and textile art, embossing, sewing, braiding, and woodworking in the enthralling actions of a dramatic performance entitled Craft Alchemy.

A prime example of creative enthusiasm and the profitable joining of forces is Fendi's live Stereo Craft show that amazed Design Miami vistors: US rock band OK Go played

1 | PP. 20 – 21
Olafur Eliasson for BMW
Your Mobile Expectations, 2007

Photography: Studio Olafur Eliasson

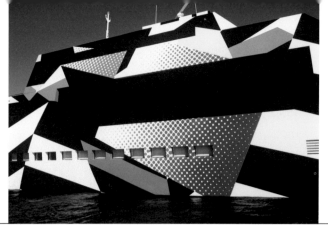

Gibson guitars customized with Fendi leather and fur, and lighting features were created by London-based tech-designer Moritz Waldemeyer. Many brands, like Fendi, appear to just know creative talent when they see it. Attempting to support and become a platform for upcoming artists, these brands garner the approval of various creative disciplines, even that of the so-called "fine" arts. The line between high and low culture fades.

There are also cases in which artists add a hint of effortless sophistication to the consumer market—introducing sculptural displays or goods of high cultural or artistic value. We marvel at Gerry Judah's large-scale installations for some of the world's leading car makers. We are invited to eat our cake off Cindy Sherman's plates and stub out our cigarettes into Damien Hirst's ashtrays.

Less elite, and therefore anchored in bread-and-butter practicalities, Trigger Happy Productions' igloo project for the German green energy supplier Entega astounded with its wit—making us step back and rethink things. Translating the company's core values into a public walk-in installation of discarded refrigerators, the clever low-cost marketing solution fostered ecological awareness and was, as ample media coverage illustrated, as promotionally effective as it was unorthodox.

Apart from its palpable surreal scenes, we witness branding becoming a promise, an experience, and a memory. Corporate environments, skillfully orchestrated by cutting-edge creatives, offer inspiring and ownable brand experiences. We enter the unchartered waters of Bompas &

Parr, paddling on an oversized bowl of over four tons of Courvoisier Cognac punch, or getting tipsy breathing in vaporized Hendrick's Gin. We live to see and sense the fine taste of fashion, if we're amongst the happy few to be invited to Stella McCartney's dinner party, designed and elaborately staged by Fiona Leahy and team. The brand experience here communicates not only ambition, but also the personal and social benefits of association.

Collectively, these examples range between a wide variety of forms, and are the subject of compelling and unique exploration into brand communication as a creative playground for experimentation within the commercial world. All blur borders, whether they find themselves at the intersection between "high" and "low" culture, or at the place between the brand's capabilities and consumers' lives. Their avant-garde spirit eschews mediocrity and appreciates profiles outside the norm. The accent is really on our sensations. There are neither pre-requisities nor rules for innovative solutions, and no recipes or guarantees for their successful implementation. As with creativity in general, it is first and foremost an intuitive decision-making process—and often a balancing act, juggling between cult value and market value, sacred and secular, distraction and contemplation, savoir-faire and savoir-vendre.

As a compilation of this kind, there are no precursors to this volume either. At the end of each marketing book, there are references for all the quotations and material brought up in the text, which is mostly descriptive and theoretical; no efforts are made to visually explore the methods portrayed as part of business practice.

Taken by Surprise compiles some of the creative approaches that are reflective of the world of branding today. It is not so much about evaluating, but about observing a situation: the status quo of the world of marketing and brand communications that is apparently flowering as never before. The wide range of modalities and corporate tools portrayed here makes us wonder: What is branding? What is art? What are the responsibilities of corporate communication? What are its limits? To what extent is the immense accumulation of spectacles a curse? Or a blessing in regard to interdisciplinary creative production? This book can only give a glimpse of what is out there, and is likely to raise more questions than it can possibly answer. We are, in fact, supposed to wonder.

2 | PP. 213 – 215
Porfiristudio × Jeff Koons
× Various Artists
Guilty, 2008

Design Concept: Ivana Porfiri
Photography: Andrea Ferrari

Joint Forces

Creative Collaboration—
Meeting of Styles and Skills

2

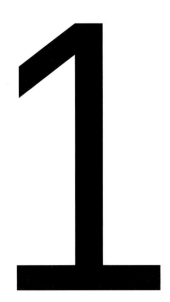

The majority of projects compiled in this book are the products of collaborative work. Capable of projecting highly accurate messages to very particular target groups, and often comprising deliberate acts of brand positioning or repositioning, the concept of collaboration is certainly one of the most important trends in contemporary brand communication. The examples gathered in this section represent special alliances—insofar as they employ established signature styles in particularly deliberate and often blatant ways.

If Absolut Vodka, BMW, or Casio teams up with Krink,
PP. 26–33 the artist's distinct dripping technique becomes the brand's marketing strategy. Whether the product produced is a watch, a car, or a limited edition vodka bottle, the Krink style remains recognizable, implying a certain subcultural relevance and thus serving its purpose as a tool for deliberate product positioning. In a similar vein, the Crystal Collection that Karl Lagerfeld   PP. 34–35 designed for Swedish glassmakers Orrefors is marked by the designer's typical black-and-white elegance, appealing to contemporary fashion enthusiasts and artisan glassware collectors alike. Therefore, it is not surprising that the knitwear and accessories collection that artist Liam Gillick
PP. 14–15   designed for Pringle of Scotland is boldly geometric in style, not to mention the fact that it is complemented with architectural interventions and a variety of exhibition formats that reference the artist's discursive mode of practice.

Based on a public proclamation of allegiance and on a certain (more or less evident) spiritual kinship, collaborations bring along a range of opportunities. Brand × brand collaborations tend to concentrate on the crossover of industry sectors, the merging of different disciplines, and the symbiosis of two or more distinctive skill sets. Brands that get together with celebrated avant-garde artists and designers enjoy the benefit of ambitious creative solutions that help them stay current.

The notion of branding as a cultural happening allows companies to stress their contemporaneity, creative relevance, and close alliance with the art world in one breath. Furthermore, the connection formed by these motives is more profound than profit. Designers and artists, on the other hand, get the chance to address the masses, explore specialist workshops and production techniques, and to work for good money on the basis of a large budget.

1

8

Structured around the nebulous and often contradictory hierarchies of fame, credibility, and affiliation, the concept of art collaboration seems to be on the rise, turning trade fairs into cultural mass events and gallery walls into sales displays. The increased recognition of the art world that effective team-ups entail is highly desirable, especially for luxury brands, whose core market

is said to have considerable overlaps with that of the art business. Indeed, a large group of well-heeled fine art collectors appear to enjoy exclusive accessories too.

While the arts, especially the so-called fine ones, are often considered the territory of the elite, advocating a position above other cultural forms and looking down on branded and functional design, commercial projects appear to gain recognition and creative approval. The spirit of the Bauhaus or the Arts and Crafts movement shines through, also in terms of multidisciplinarity.

A range of brands such as Fendi, Missoni, Swarovski, Baccarat, and Colette, have come to be seen as experimental platforms for newcomer artists and designers. Furthermore, realizing that artists not only "arise," but are often in fact created by those who support their work, art lovers are much obliged. Creative patronage and the nurturing of new and up-and-coming artists are not just ways for brands to emphasize their own cultural importance; it also garners huge buzz for the brand, for the product, and for the artist—especially online, where information flows quicker than anywhere else.

But the modern consumer is known to be jaded and critical. By far, most collaborations will not peak consumer interested. The most striking examples appear to be based on true partnership, not the mere link-up of service providers and creative patrons. Once the right partner is found, collaborative success depends on shared values and a real understanding of each other's identity and heritage. Respectfulness, mutual trust, and understanding are also crucial.

Many brands, like the ones mentioned above, move easily between various creative spheres, working with fine artists, architects, writers and film-makers, and they keep coming up with exciting new projects. On the other hand, many artists, like Damien Hirst, Krink, and David Lynch, can move easily between commercial spheres, working on a range of projects without losing credibility and recognition within their respective creative fields.

There are also artists who turn the tables by pulling the commercial work they do for brands into their artistic oeuvre, like Takashi Murakami did with his Louis Vuitton paintings, which consist of nothing but the multicolored LV pattern he originally created on commission from the French deluxe accessory makers. This example illustrates the dynamism of collaboration that this section aims to reflect. The flexibility and versatility of creative alliance is a source of inspiration for many disciplines. Signature styles become strategies, and symbiotic synergies become the driving forces of creative communication.

PP. 10–13
Erwin Wurm
**Advertising Campaign (unpublished),
1997**
—

Asked by the lingerie company Palmers to create advertisements for a campaign, Erwin Wurm created a series of 12 photographs showing the body of a woman undressing herself. Unlike his previous sculptures incorporating pullovers or T-shirts, which depicted bodies concealed or truncated, this series was perceived as much more sexually provocative. Since it was significantly more charged than previous Palmers campaigns, Wurm's project was not accepted by Palmers and the campaign was never realized.

Photography: Studio Wurm   Courtesy: Gallery Thaddaeus Ropac, Salzburg, Austria

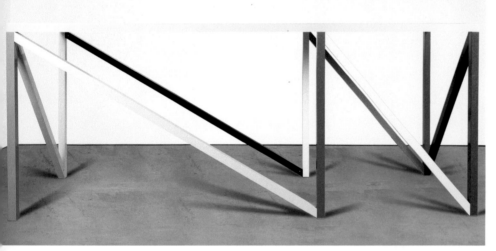

Liam Gillick
× Pringle of Scotland
LiamGillickforPringleofScotland, 2011

British conceptual artist Liam Gillick and Pringle of Scotland's Creative Director Alistair Carr have created an accessories and knitwear capsule collection labeled LiamGillickforPringleofScotland. The collection remains true to Gillick's signature style, taking its starting point from a series of abstract color block permutations by the artist, and incorporates a bright palette of contrasting colors offset with black and grey.

As a preview, Gillick created an intervention on runway benches for Pringle's womenswear show at London fashion week in September 2011. The typographic piece was made from fragments from Gillick's book Construction of One. The full collection was unveiled a month later in a custom pop-up shop at Art Basel Miami Beach.

liamgillickforpringleofscotland

15

Pharrell Williams for Domeau & Pérès
Perspective Chair, 2008

Designed by Pharrell Williams in collaboration with Domeau & Pérès, the Perspective Chair is the product of deep personal involvement with fundamental life experiences. Williams says: "I had often wondered what it's like to truly be in love, not just for once... So I decided not to ask what it was like in someone else's shoes or what it was like to sit in their seat... I decided to sketch out my own experiment; the perspective chair."

Domeau & Pérès created Williams's experiment in four colors: red, yellow, black, and blue. The chair is made of tinted resin, its seat is covered with leather. From a limited edition of eight per color, one set was put on display at Galerie Emmanuel Perrotin.

Photography: Benoit Fougeirol
Gallery: Galerie Emmanuel Perrotin

1

1
...,staat for
Bugaboo × Missoni
Bugaboo meets Missoni Special
Collection, 2011

Always on the lookout for unexpected and exciting collaborations, Bugaboo partnered with Italian fashion house Missoni to outfit Bugaboo's classic strollers with the knitwear pioneer's iconic patterns. Based on a creative concept by ...,staat, a collection of two tailored designs and a knitted blanket were created, all manufactured in Italy along the lines of Missoni's signature style.

The collaboration is accompanied by an optical illusion movie that merges the two worlds of Bugaboo and Missoni within a custom built op-art inspired setting, with music by Monk Higgins.

Concept & Art Direction: ...,staat Creative Agency   Photography: Barrie Hullegie & Sabrina Bongiovanni   Styling: Maarten Spruyt

2
Scott Campbell for Pirelli
Pirelli Zero P, 2011

For tire makers Pirelli, tattoo artist Scott Campbell turned his needle to rubber and etched a montage of skull, heart, and eye into the tread of a Pirelli Diablo Rosso II tire. The artist's style was applied to an exclusive Dainese motorcycle jacket, and the special tire was fitted to a special-edition Ducati Diavel to be put on show at Pirelli's Milan flagship store.

2

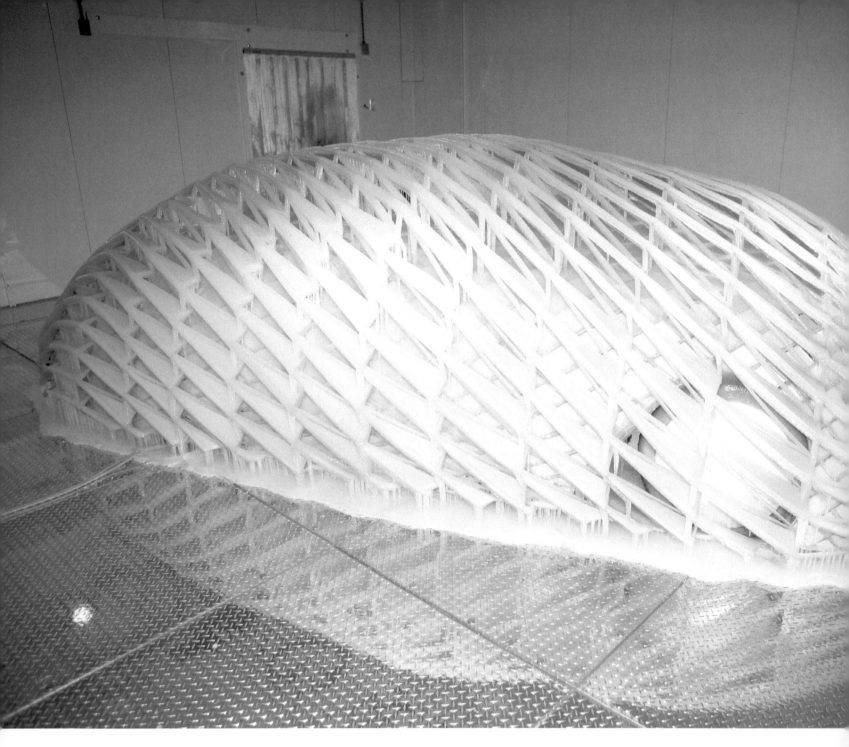

Olafur Eliasson for BMW
Your Mobile Expectations, 2007

BMW commissioned Olafur Elias-son to develop a research project on the basis of a hydrogen-powered BMW H2R. Scrutinizing the car not as an object, but as part of a complex set of relations and exchanges with its surroundings, the conceptual artist engaged in a series of conversations with architects, scientists, designers, and theorists, and investigated surfaces, patterns, and structures according to how they relate to movement and perspective.

After establishing a rich pool of relevant background information, Eliasson conducted various tests with ice in a custom-made yellow geodesic dome in the garden of his studio. These tests resulted in a double-layer skin consisting of welded steel rods and mirrors, which was based on spiral geometry. Onto this intricate structure about 2,000 liters of water were sprayed, freezing into a skin of icicles. Intrinsically tied to the conditions of its surroundings, the outlandish sculpture was designed to exist only in a special freezing environment. Lit by monofrequency light, the piece glowed mystically from within.

Photography: Studio Olafur Eliasson

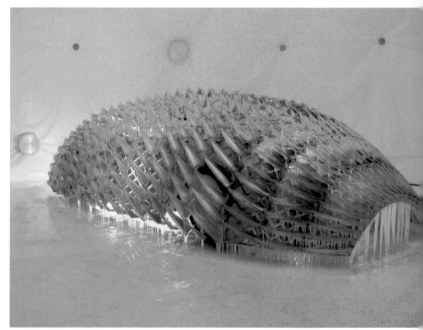

Maybach × Julian Schnabel
The Ones You Didn't Write, 2011

Since 2010, Julian Schnabel and Maybach have been engaging in a multitude of collaborative initiatives.

One highlight of this relationship was the presentation of the Maybach sculpture Queequeg in front of the New World Symphony building during Art Basel Miami. Another product of their collaboration was the custom-designed Maybach Saloon entitled The Ones You Didn't Write. The idea for the project evolved in the context of Schnabel's involvement in the Wilhelm & Karl Maybach Foundation's mentoring program, an initiative that supports young and talented artists. The result of this involvement was the creation of a fascinating art piece that was moored on the Grand Canal during the Venice Biennale 2011. The pink-lettered car riddled with numerous bullet holes turned many heads at the art event.

The auto body was expressively painted by Julian Schnabel, and the inside windows were pasted up with drawings by the artist's protégé Vahakn Arslanian.

Photography: Daimler AG

Rolf Sachs for Smart
Smart Fortwo Sprinkle, 2010

Commissioned to design an art car
for Smart, Swiss artist Rolf Sachs re-
sorted to his distinctive splashing and
marking technique. Vivid colors, paint
splatters and even the designer's own
handprint make for an overall look that
complements the free-spirited, young,
and creative image of the car. The interior is a motley arrangement of colored
patches, buttons, and off-stitching. The
Sprinkle was unveiled as a unique piece
at Milan Design Week 2010.

Tom Sachs for Colette
Trunk Store, 2010

Renowned for his unexpected reinterpretation of readily available objects, New York-based artist Tom Sachs partnered with Colette to present the Trunk Show, an assortment of subversively humorous goods. His "Store" was a mobile display trunk showcasing a selection of rare collector's items, functional objects, and publications that the artist produced over the last few years. Amongst them were the famous Sharpie, the "Stanley Kubrick is Dead" measuring tape, the KRINK marker set, and the Nutsy's Deluxe Racing Set, which was a ready-to-start remote-controlled car set manufactured by Kyosho Electronics.

Colette sold every piece in the trunk, both in the store and online.

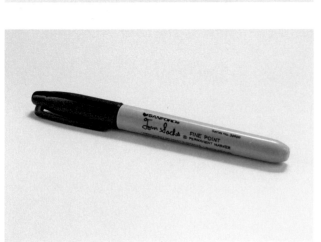

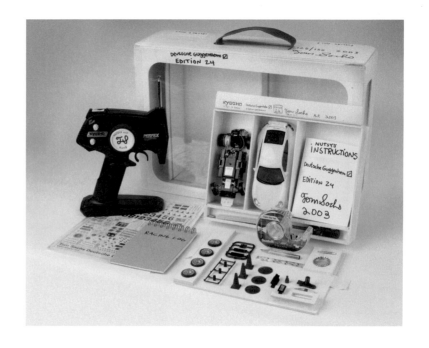

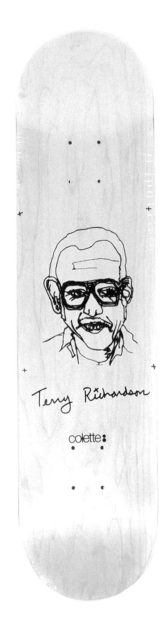

Terry Richardson × Colette
Mom/Dad, 2011

Parisian boutique extraordinaire Colette presented a range of exclusive releases celebrating Terry Richardson's Mom/Dad exhibition. The collaborative series includes T-shirts, skateboards, and necklaces, plus a nicely packaged set of Baby-G watches that Casio produced exclusively for the collaboration. All products were inspired by the photographer's signature flannel shirts, and made available at Colette's store, as well as a specialty Richardson merchandise pop-up e-store on the Colette website.

1

Typically, street artists appear to work in an atmosphere remote from—or even opposed to—the fluctuating trends of the consumer industry. The New York-based artist Craig Costello, a.k.a. Krink, is one of the very few who has achieved global celebrity status, both in the commercial and sub-cultural environmnent. He achieves this not by switching back and forth between worlds, but by wisely defining his own.

Done right, creative collaboration is full of opportunities. From the brand perspective, that means acceptance in a particular field of arts or a certain interest group—in Krink's case, the international street art community—along with the brands. Good collaborative projects have this connection that is generally obvious. If they don't, it's a reason to turn down the project. We were recently approached by a car company, and I felt they had no idea what they were doing, no concept of what the audience was interested in, they were just too big to see anything outside of their cubicle. The car was awful. They had no concept whatsoever about urban culture or style, and it was sad. When we did the Mini, the person who approached us understood the Krink brand. He actually made the effort to get around his large company's bureaucracy to make it happen. He took a risk, because he knew it would be well received. And it was."

"The Mini is a design classic with a history in an urban environment," Costello goes on to say. As a matter of fact, his

"Through graffiti I learned a lot about placement and how someone might view something, like painting something really big that's meant to be viewed from far away. With branding and marketing, I learned that often when people want something, you just have to give it to them."

various benefits of association that entails. New customer groups may be targeted almost unerringly and, along the way, the product range gains ambitious creative solutions and at best takes share in the well-received and unique style of the collaborator.

Krink's signature style is a paradigm in continuity and distinction. The visual language of the New York-based artist is based on his signature dripping technique. Interested in street culture and trying to reach out to it, many commercial clients want the iconic Krink drips. Not all get them.

Knowing that every collaboration is a creative statement on either side, Craig Costello operates with clarity and foresight. As an artist, he has allows himself to be selective. As a brand, Krink has an assertive corporate strategy. "We are careful about how we portray ourselves, and people appreciate that. It's very important to have a connection between brands working together. The collaboration should make sense; there should be a story or connection that is relevant to both

creative partnerships that work are known to be based on common ground: Krink × Mini, Krink × Tom Sachs, Krink × Casio, Krink × Incase.

But if the × in collaboration stands for crossing roads, it certainly stands for crossing borders, too. The border between industries and target groups, for example, or the border between art and product design. While many artists from various creative backgrounds hold onto the claim that art should never sell itself for advertising, Craig Costello has sensibly established a body of work that balances his personal creative vision with the commercial requirements of the brands he works with. Understanding art as a relative term, he points at its intrinsic relation to commercial interest. "The art world is a business that treats artwork like commodities, and artists like companies with market share and prices. Buy low, sell high, supply and demand. Artists need to position themselves well, laugh at jokes, and sacrifice like anyone else. So in the end, in a capitalist culture, it's what you buy or don't buy, sell or don't sell."

Instead of worrying about the issue of commercialization, Krink focuses on process. Treating the Mini Cooper more like a sculptural piece, he refers to most of his other collaborations as design projects. Whatever they are, they are all intrinsically tied to his background as a graffiti artist. After all, graffiti works a bit like brand marketing. He says, "I only realized the parallels after I was exposed to marketing and working with a brand. It's about the projection of ideas, style, placement. It's a completely different angle, but in some ways very similar."

1 | P. 24
Krink × Tom Sachs
Custom Markers, 2010

Photography: Tom Sachs

Krink × Mini
Krink Mini, 2008

BMW entrusted the artist Craig Costello, also known as KR or by his brand name Krink, to drop his silver ink all over a new black Mini Cooper S. Treating the Mini's iconic shape as a sculptural object, Krink created a unique art car, resplendent in an array of splatters and drips.

The project was unveiled at the Erste Liebe Bar in Hamburg before becoming part of an urban art exhibition at Vicious Gallery, also in Hamburg.

Photography: Ali Salehi

1
Krink × Uniform Experiment
Tote Bags, 2011

On the occasion of the fashion label Sophnet's 12th anniversary, its sublabel Uniform Experiment got together with Krink to work on a series of collaborative products. Amongst these were 12 signed and numbered tote bags, hand-painted by the artist using his signature drippy style.

Photography: Uniform Experiment

2
Krink × Arkitip × Incase
Laptop Sleeve, 2009

The Apple product sleeve makers at Incase launched the Curated by Arkitip project in accordance with the brand's relentless commitment to design. The first signature piece within the line was the Krink Laptop Sleeve, a refined version of the classic sleeve that merges KR's artistry with Incase's clutter-free design and lasting durability.

Photography: Incase

1

"People view the Krink brand and style as unique and interesting. I've been very fortunate to have the opportunity to work with some great companies. I like their products and their style."

2

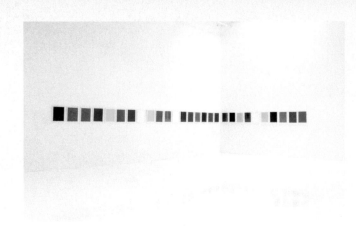

1

2

"It's good to break rules and cross boundaries. There's a lot of opportunity to make interesting things, and that's also an important part of collaborative projects."

1 2 3
Krink × Casio
18 Wooster, 2011

Staying true to both G-Shock's bold approach and Krink's celebrated dripping technique, the special edition DW6900KR-8 watch features a full mirror-face and a custom matte silver finish. A privately hosted launch event at New York's Wooster Street celebrated the release of the watch. KR painted two large walls of the space, and 28 framed monochrome artworks completed the installation.

Photography: Craig Costello[1],
Jason Lewis[2,3]

4
Krink × Agnès B.
Storefront, 2010

When French clothing line Agnès B. opened its new boutique in New York City's SoHo district, the label commissioned Craig Costello, a.k.a. Krink, to design a women's tank top and to cover the storefront with his iconic drips.

Photography: Craig Costello

3, 4 ^{opposite page}

**Krink × EXIT Magazine
× Absolut Vodka**

A Work in Progress, 2010

One notable project within the extensive series of Absolut limited edition art bottles, and one result of the the long-standing symbiosis between the vodka brand and the fashion and photography magazine EXIT, Krink customized 15 unique Absolut Glimmer patterned crystal bottles. The project was commissioned by both the famous spirit makers and EXIT editor Stephen Toner.

EXIT magazine chose one of the drippy bottles to adorn the cover of its fall/winter issue, and documented the making-of in an editorial feature.

Photography: Bjorn Iooss

"Krink is a brand that represents a creative community. People see that I work on creative projects and am not a giant faceless corporation. I think this has been really important."

Portrait

Krink

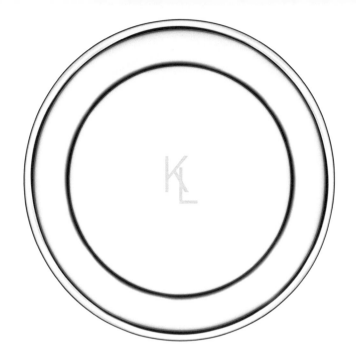

After all the fashion, perfumes, and accessories, Karl Lagerfeld released his first line of crystal in collaboration with the traditional Swedish artisan glassmakers at Orrefors. Understanding the artistic excellence of Orrefors as comparable with the world of high fashion, Karl Lagerfeld designed a line of crystal in his own image: clean-lined, subtle, and functional.

The collection includes champagne flutes and coupes, as well as wine, water, and liqueur glasses. The pieces are transparent, black, or milky white, and some are engraved with the KL monogram. The collection includes monogrammed coasters to prevent any trace of an errant drop on an immaculate tablecloth, in accordance with the spirit of the designer's well-known practicality.

Photography: Jonas Lindström, Karl Lagerfeld

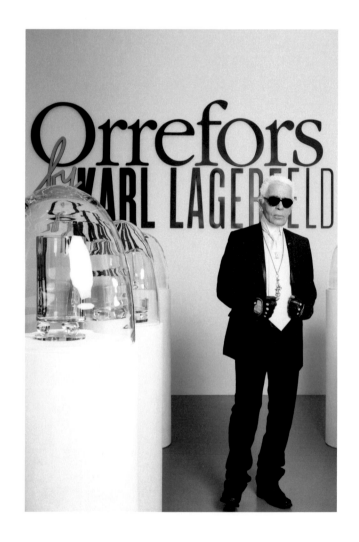

Baccarat × ECAL
Harcourt Glassware, 2011

Baccarat's iconic Harcourt glassware reached its 170th anniversary in 2011, and the original forms of the pieces had never been altered until then. Entrusted with Harcourt's very first reinterpretation, students of the Master of Advanced Studies in Luxury Industry and Design program at ECAL Lausanne revived the art of crystal glassmaking.

The students' new designs celebrate the Harcourt style with a contemporary twist. Daniel Martinez's collection of bracelets in lacquer and silver is based on horizontal slices in the shape of Harcourt glass. Decha Archjananun's set of cup and ball games consists of modified Harcourt elements. Elsa Lambinet stretched the form of the Harcourt glass, creating a metaphor of the longevity of this 170-year-old shape. Fumiko Ito's lollipop riffs on the Harcourt's characteristic flat cut, and Xin Wang designed a series of glasses with modified feet that, once turned upside down, becomes a chess game.

Based on these prototypes, which the students created during a workshop led by British designers Ed Barber and Jay Osgerby, the collection was produced by Baccarat's craftsmen and put on display at Milan Design Week 2011.

Photography: ECAL/Julien Chavaillaz

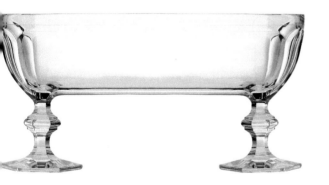

1
Stählemühle × Tim Lee
Tonite's the Day, 2007

Canadian artist Tim Lee designed his Stählemühle Schnapps Edition along the lines of of his first German solo exhibition at Galerie Rüdiger Schöttle in Munich. Made from fully ripe fruits according to a traditional recipe, the type of genuine apricot schnapps in the bottles Lee designed, called "Ungarische Beste" ("Best of Hungary"), from the Lake Balaton area, celebrates the the year 2022 in advance. It pays tribute to the particularly long storage potential of the distilled liquor, and to the inextricable relationship of conceptual art with the phenomena of time in general. Lee's label design for his edition of 50 bottles takes on this theme in terms of precise typographical implementation.

2
Stählemühle × Jonathan Meese
Getreidedaddy Doppelkorn, 2007

This double-distilled schnapps tastes like bread, wheat, and revolution. Originally distilled for the German artist Jonathan Meese's Getreidedaddy Bar, which was part of an installation Meese set up within the scope of the 2007 special-exhibition Remarx at Karl Marx Museum in Trier, the schnapps celebrates wheat as a form of social authority and as an object of "absolute revolutionary capability" (to quote Meese). The title Getreidedaddy refers to no one less than Karl Marx himself. The project is accompanied by a book about Marx, art, and the future of revolution by Meese, edited by Robert Eikmeyer, the curator of the Remarx Exhibition, and Christoph Keller of Edelobstbrennerei Stählemühle.

A limited edition of 100 0.7-liter bottles were each numbered and signed by the artist.

3
Heideggerz Schwarzwaelder Kirsch, 2008

Edelobstbrennerei Stählemühle distilled this Black Forest kirsch on the occasion of a "Feldwegwanderung" (dirt track tramp), initiated and spearheaded by the artist Jonathan Meese, in honor of Martin Heidegger's Todtnauberger Hütte in the Black Forest. In the company of the art critic Wolfgang Ullrich, actor Martin Wuttke, the Remarx curator Robert Eikmeyer, and a couple of others, Meese stopped in at a little ski hut not far from the philosopher's famous cottage and probably had a few glasses.

Heideggerz Schwarzwaelder Kirsch has been produced in an edition of 66 0.5-liter bottles, each designed, signed, and numbered by Jonathan Meese.

5
Stählemühle × Jonathan Monk
The Merry Monk, 2007

British artist Jonathan Monk created a work of conceptual and autobiographical word-play for Stählemühle. The Merry Monk stands as a symbol for peaceable, untroubled devotion, and blissful intoxication caused by this genuine apricot schnapps. On the label, the monk appears inanimate, in form of a stylized epitaph. The birth date on the epigraph is Monk's. There is no death date; in its stead is a handwritten note by the artist: "Until then, Jonathan." This message is written on all 66 signed and numbered bottles.

2

3

4

5
Stählemühle
× Stefan Marx
Nancy is Okay, 2010

Nancy is Okay is the most recent of Stählemühle's Artist Editions. The edition is based on the Mirabelle de Nancy, a special type of plum that Hamburg-based Artist Stefan Marx took as the inspiration for an extensive series of small-format drawings. One hundred unique artworks were printed on one hundred bottles of fine 2010 apricot schnapps, at the highly-awarded distillery of Edelobstbrennerei, Stählemühle's family business.

5

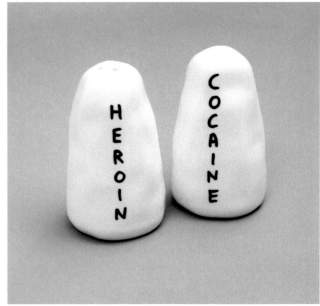

David Shrigley for Polite
Salt and Pepper Shakers and Plectrums, 2008/2009

With the mission to make "the witty, wonderful world of contemporary art a bit easier to come by," Polite collaborates with creatives to produce and distribute very special but affordable products. One of their longest working relationships is with British artist David Shrigley. Out of the wide variety of projects the designers have created with Shrigley, two of Polite's favorites are the guitar plectrums and the salt and pepper shakers. Both were developed from ideas by the artist. The salt and pepper shakers are made using fine bone china at a traditional Staffordshire pottery, and are presented in handmade boxes.

3

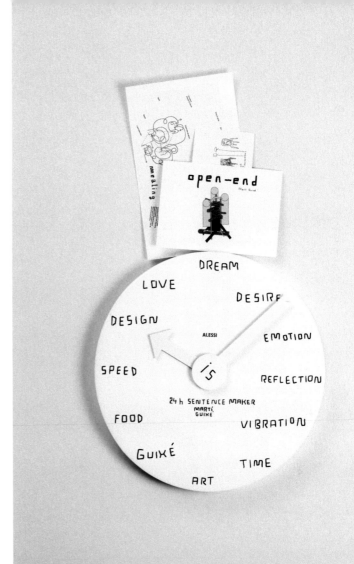

4

3
Alessi × Martí Guixé
Blank Wall Clock and 24h Sentence Maker, 2010

Alessi and Martí Guixé together comprise one of leading brands of contemporary design and one of the key figures of contemporary design criticism. Dubbing himself an "ex-designer," Martí Guixé criticizes the discipline for its formalistic, stylized approach. Instead of seeking new forms for already existing typologies, Martí Guixé is on a quest for new perspectives and new interpretations of everyday objects. Alberto Alessi describes Guixé's work as by no means moralizing, but rather playful and pleasantly paradoxical. Key to this play is the involvement of an active user—and the Blank Wall Clock is no exception.

Guixé's clock plays on the idea of time as a subjective and highly individual phenomenon, inviting the user to customize its blank face to his or her liking. The impermanent marker allows for a myriad of redesigns. The clock hands, which are also constantly changing, form a complete arrow when aligned.

The design of the 24h Sentence Maker is very similar, with the difference that the hours are indicated on this model. The moving arrow made up of second and minute hands creates and recreates a multitude of temporary word combinations, linked by the "is" on the arrows' hinge: what reads "Design is Emotion" at 10:10 am, becomes "Guixé is Art" at 7:30 pm.

4
Alessi × Martí Guixé
Seed Safe, 2010

The Seed Safe is a box for saving plant seeds. Another collaboration between Alessi and Martí Guixé, and another example of the self-appointed "ex-designer's" playful approach to meaningful and responsible product development, this one-of-a-kind kitchen good calls attention to the fact that not only animal species are threatened by extinction, but that so are many kinds of fruits and vegetables. Borrowing its name from the "seed-savers," organizations that gather and archive the seeds of endangered plant species, this stoneware container encourages private households to do the same—or at least to become more attentive to the flora and fauna in their everyday surroundings.

Photography: Inga Knölke [3,4]

Hand-study

Geoff McFetridge for Heath Ceramics

My Head Disappears When My Hands Are Thinking, 2011

Longtime friends, the Los Angeles-based graphic artist and illustrator Geoff McFetridge and the Heath Ceramics LA Studio Director Adam Silverman finally realized their long-standing intention to collaborate. The result was a complete custom-painted dinnerware set with McFetridge's iconic line drawings and paintings, including service accessories for six people, a hand-carved teapot and cup sets, and custom hand-carved vases in both one-of-a-kind and limited-edition multiples.

The seven-week show My Head Disappears When My Hands Are Thinking at Heath Ceramics Los Angeles Studio & Showroom highlighted McFetridge's interest in decoration, his idea of drawing as meditation, and his growing interest in crafting physical things. The Heath project was Geoff McFetridge's very first experience working with clay.

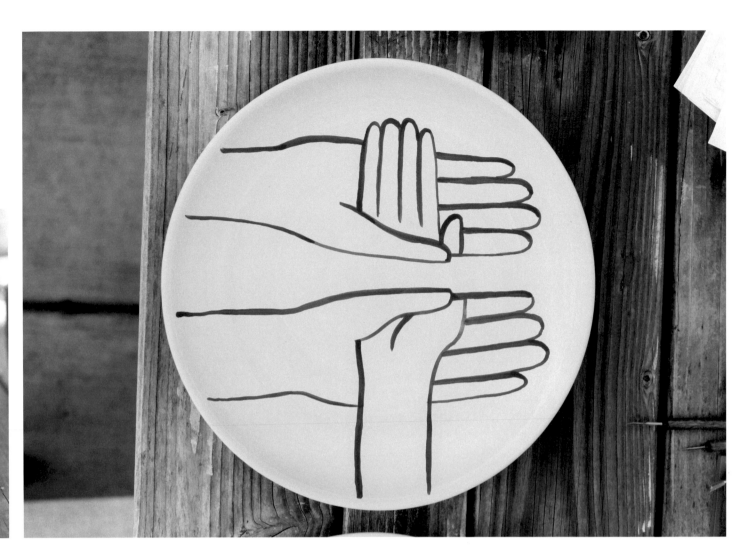

Hayon Studio × Maruwakaya for Kutani Choemon
Ceramics Edition, 2010

Blurring the lines between art, craft, and decoration, as he has done so many times before before, Spanish designer Jaime Hayon linked up with the Japanese product design brand Maruwakaya to create a lovingly-executed edition of ceramics for the traditional Japanese artisan pottery Kutani Choemon.

A tribute to the richness of Japanese dinner table culture, the multifaceted collection consists of over ten pieces, all handmade in Kamide Choemon's workshop by dint of original Japanese techniques.

Photography: Nienke Klunder

Hayon Studio for Swarovski
Sparkle Cabinet and Chandelier, 2007

These two twinkling limited-edition pieces were manufactured by Hayon Studio in collaboration with Swarovski. The chandelier consists of a series of different lampshades, and although its structure is fixed once set up, it is possible to choose between several styles, sizes, colors, and materials of lampshade. A multitude of Swarovski crystals, hot-fixed onto the textile and then fitted over the shades, allows for an amazing game of light, even when the lamps are not lit.

The multi-leg cabinet, originally part of Jaime Hayón's 2005 Showtime collection for the Spanish firm BD Ediciones de Diseño, took cues from the glittery setting of MGM musicals. The sparkle version is covered with 5,600 Swarovski crystals, applied to its surface entirely by hand.

Photography: Nienke Klunder

Hayon Studio for Lladró
Fantasy Collection, 2008

The fruitful alliance of Jamie Hayon and the Spanish artisan porcelain brand Lladró began back in 2005, culminating with the artist's appointment as the brand's creative adviser. Their joint venture, entitled Fantasy Collection, is a celebration of the unexpected, based on illusion and innovation. Believing in the power of creative collaboration, both the artist and the brand describe the project as a "perfect fusion" between the maximum expression of what can be achieved in porcelain and the touches of fantasy coming from Jamie Hayón's own personal world. The collection was launched against the backdrop of the Milan Furniture Fair 2008.

Photography: Nienke Klunder

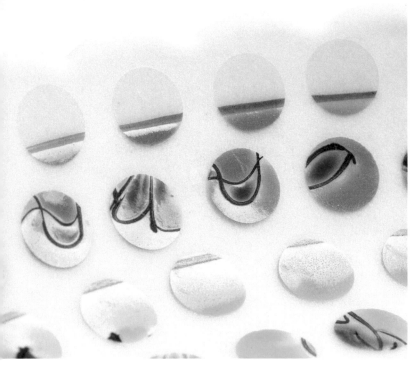

Hans Tan Studio for FARM
Spotted Nyonya, 2011

Spotted Nyonya is an industrial re-interpretation of Nyonya porcelain vessels, which are traditional domestic

wares native to Chinese Peranakans in Southeast Asia. Hans Tan Studio's contemporary take on the traditional style transforms the vessels' original mul-

ticolored surface into a new dot pattern, using a technique similar in concept to the resist-dyeing technique that is often applied to dyed fabric patterns. The porcelain pieces are masked with a new dot motif, which is then sandblasted, preserving the glaze in protected areas while erasing the glazed sections from exposed areas and revealing the white porcelain that lies beneath. Produced and distributed by Farm, the first series of Spotted Nyonya was awarded the inventive product award "Les Découvertes" as part of the "Now! Design à vivre" show at the the fall edition of Maison&Objet 2011 in Paris.

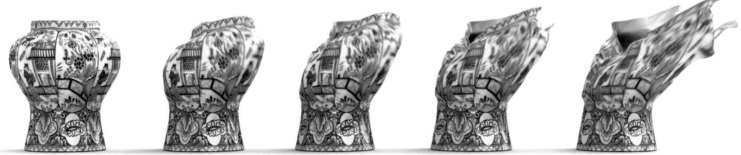

1

1

Front for Moooi
Blow Away Vase, 2008

Designed by Swedish design team Front for the Dutch company Moooi, this royal blue Delft vase looks as if it has been blown away by a strong gust of wind during the manufacturing process. Combining traditional painting techniques with bold experimentation and digital manipulation, the handmade and therefore unique sculptural ceramic pieces are produced by Royal Delft Porcelain Manufacture, just as their classic archetypes.

distributed via Editions in Craft, an international creative platform that focuses on traditional crafts and specialized manufacturing.

Photography: Anna Lönnerstam

2

Front × The Siyazama Project for Editions in Craft
Story Vases, 2010

The Siyazama Project is a collective of women working with traditional bead crafts in KwaZulu-Natal, South Africa. This long-term conceptual design project began with a series of conversations in Durban, South Africa, between Anna, Sofia, and Charlotte of Front Design and Beauty, and Thokozani, Kishwepi, Tholiwe, and Lobolile of the Siyazama Project. The vases are inspired by the lives of the five South African women, who formed their personal stories into text by threading glass beads onto metal wires. Using traditional glassblowing techniques, their vase-shaped wire molds were then turned into vases to be

Lacoste × Li Xiaofeng
The Porcelain Polo Holiday Collector's Series, 2010

For its 2010 Holiday Collector's Series, Lacoste asked the Chinese Artist Li Xiaofeng to reinvent the iconic L.12.12 polo shirt. The artist obliged with an original sculpture that served as the inspiration for an exclusive print to be used in a complementary series of limited-edition polos.

and polished as usual, and then photographed to be digitized and used as elements of the intricate design; however, the Polo sculpture is made using new, custom shards. Inspired by the early Ming Dynasty, Li Xiaofeng painted porcelain bowls with both traditional Chinese floral motifs and lettering, as well

A trained muralist, Li Xiaofeng's recent work is mainly sculptural, and consists of shards of broken porcelain recovered from ancient archeological digs. He shapes and polishes them, and then drills holes to link the pieces together with silver wire, creating what he calls "rearranged landscapes." For the Porcelain Polo artwork, the artist slightly adapted his method. The polo designs are based on blue and white shards from the Kangxi Period of the Qing Dynasty that the artist shaped

as the Lacoste crocodile logo and brand name. After three months of painting, firing, fragmenting, shaping, polishing, and finally linking together, the polo was ready to be unveiled in Paris at the Musée des Arts et Métiers, and then again in Beijing within the framework of Li Xiaofeng's first solo show organized by the Red Gate Gallery.

1
Alessandro Mendini for Bisazza
Poltrona di Proust Monumentale, 2005

The Italian luxury decorators at Bisazza and the artist Alessandro Mendini are united by over twenty years of collaboration and a creative dialogue based on common interest and aesthetic affinity. One of the results of their symbiotic partnership is the famous Poltrona di Proust, a re-design of the original 1978 Proust Armchair. The polychrome color pattern of the oversized 2005 version has been applied using a technique called divisionism. Mendini himself describes the piece as a collage: the piece's form is that of a baroque, romantic armchair, and the infinite hand-brushed strokes on the chair's surface are inspired by a detail from a meadow painted by the French artist Paul Signac.

Photography: Alberto Ferrero

2
Lacoste × Campanas Brothers
Campanas Holiday Collectors Series, 2009

Lacoste collaborated with the designers Fernando and Humberto Campana of Sao Paulo-based Estudio Campana for their 2009 Holiday Collectors Series.

Taking the iconic crocodile logo as a starting point, the Campanas Brothers designed two editions of polos, a limited and a super-limited edition, both exclusively produced in cooperation with Coopa-Roca, a socially-responsible sustainable development organization in Rio de Janeiro. There are two styles of polo available, with different arrangements of sewn croc-odile badges. The men's pieces are inspired by Anavilhanas, small fluvial islands on the Amazon, and the design of the women's shirts references the Lianas vines that grow on trees in the tropical rainforest.

Core to the concept of the collaboration is the "alligator chair," referencing the reptile's habit of piling up in mud beds during the dry season. Keeping with the overall Amazon theme, the crocodile's natural habitat inspired the setting of an elaborately-designed event staged to launch the collaborative project at Hôtel De Roquelaure in Paris in June 2009.

2

Studio Job for Bisazza
Silverware, 2007

Designed by the Dutch-Belgian duo Studio Job especially for Bisazza's Limited Editions collection, Silverware is a series that was first presented with great success during Milan Design Week 2007. Three large-scale sculptures from the eight-piece collection were then put on show at the Bisazza store in SoHo. Entirely covered in a white gold mosaic, mesmerizing in their gigantic format, the pieces captured the observers' attention and cast a unique and slightly surreal spell. The complete collection includes a cake platter, a silver spoon, a dish cover, a tea tray, a chandelier, a candle holder, a teapot, and a basket.

Photography: J.B. Mondino

1

2

3

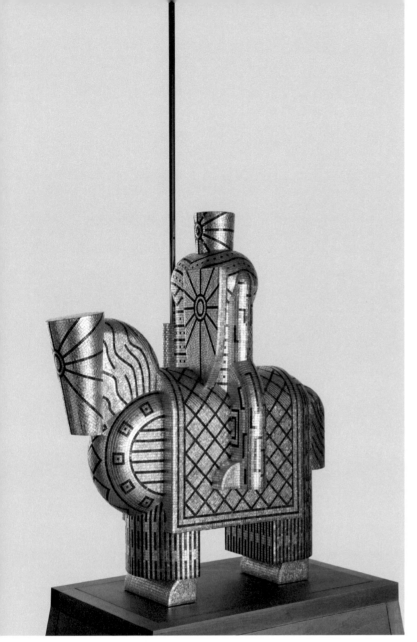

1 2 3
**Alessandro Mendini
for Bisazza**
Mobili Per Uomo, 1997 – 2009

Alessandro Mendini's series of gold glass mosaic figures for Bisazza is an extensive celebration of the long-standing and remarkable partnership between the artist and the luxury decorators. Over a period of ten years, Mendini designed nine sculptural pieces of gigantic proportions, which were decorated with hand-cut 24-karat yellow gold mosaic tiles and perched on top of unfinished galvanized iron cabinets. Entitling the collection Mobili per Uomo ("Furniture for Man"), Mendini formed each figure to represent a symbol of "contemporary man": a face, a glove, an elegant shoe, an evening jacket, a teacup, a bedside lamp, a briefcase, a Borsalino hat, and a star.

Each a part of an enduring exhibition, the pieces travel to be displayed at Bisazza's major flagship stores throughout Europe.

Photography: Marco Mignani[1],
Ottavio Tomasini[2][3]

4
**Alessandro Mendini
for Bisazza**
Il Cavaliere di Dürer, 2011

Another result of the creative partnership between Alessandro Mendini and the famous Italian mosaic makers, the Il Cavaliere di Dürer project has raised Bisazza tiles to a new level of contemporary artistry.

Inspired by Albrecht Dürer's detailed etchings and the compositional entity of horse and knight he portrayed, Mendini transposed Dürer's ancient image into glass mosaic. This new work is an imposing statue covered in blue and white cubic tesserae, in which two figures of sparkling armor seemingly blend together. The delicacy of the blue lines alludes to the masterful play of the burin carving tool in Dürer's engraving.

Photography: Lorenzo Ceretta

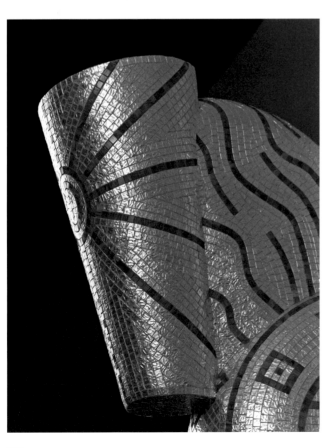

4

1
Cappellini
× Satyendra Pakhalé
Walt Disney Eco Fish, 2010

Cappellini teamed up with Walt Disney and Amsterdam-based designer Satyendra Pakhalé to create the Eco Fish signature limited edition chair. The piece is a showcase armchair for the latest advancements in fabrication, molded from a single-pour multicolor plastic element using a new rotational technique. The material is recycled to underscore Cappellini's continued focus on sustainability, and draw attention to the company's self-imposed mission of conserving raw materials for future generations. An edition of 99 numbered pieces has been produced.

2
Cappellini
× François Azambourg
Bugatti Racing Chair, 2009

The furniture industry met the world of speed when Cappellini released its Bugatti Racing Chair, a "fireball design" by François Azambourg, in 2009. A tribute to the iconic Italian race car, the armchair is lacquered in flaming red color with contrasting white stripes. The thin metal plate material that looks a bit like crumpled tin is injected with polyurethane foam. The edition is limited to 99 signed and numbered pieces.

3
Cappellini × Walt Disney
× Nendo
Mickey's Ribbon Stool, 2010

Clearly inspired by Mickey's characteristic ribbon, Cappellini, Walt Disney, and Japanese designer Nendo came up with this limited edition signature stool. With its circular shape, open design and flowing lines, the Ribbon Stool lends itself perfectly to the famous silhouette that peeks over its seat. Merging flawlessly together, the two images create a single, iconic representation as the result of a seamless collaboration. The series of high and low stools is made of laser-cut and folded sheet metal. The lower version, produced in a limited and numbered edition of 399, comes with a polished red varnish, and the high one, limited to 199 pieces, is produced in yellow with transparent plastic feet.

4
Maarten Baas for
Amnesty International
Empty Chair, 2011

Maarten Baas designed the Empty Chair upon an invitation by Amnesty International, and in honor of the Chinese Nobel Peace Prize winner Liu Xiaobo. Awarded for his peaceful battle for fundamental human rights, Liu Xiaobo could not accept the prize in person because he was in jail serving an 11-year sentence for "undermining the state." Designed to support Amnesty International's campaign against the increased suppression of writers, Baas's five-meter-tall chair became a symbol for repression, presented in Amsterdam on May 28, 2011, the 50th anniversary of Amnesty International. A miniature Empty Chair will soon be available in the form of an exclusive pin.

Photography: Frank Tielemans

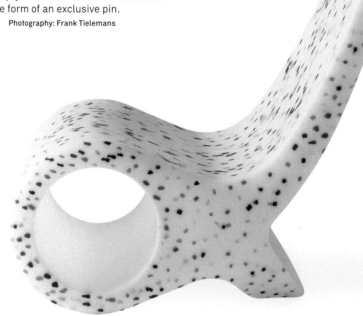

1

2

3

Kartell
Kartell loves Milano, 2011

On the occasion of the 50th Salone Internazionale del Mobile, Kartell presented Kartell loves Milano, a genuine tribute to Milan—the city that saw the company's beginnings and its successes right from its earliest stages in the 1950s.

For the project, the renowned furniture house invited 45 collaborators from diverse creative fields; from fashion to design, from art to photography, and from literature to entertainment. The collaborators were invited to pay tribute to Italy's design capital by re-imagining one of Kartell's plastic furniture designs. Among the many names of those who joined the project are the great Milanese fashion houses Missoni, Moschino, and Vhernier, and a large number of designers and architects from all over the world, such as Mario Bellini, Andrea Branzi, Alessandro Mendini, Fabio Novembre, Philippe Starck, and Tokujin Yoshioka.

The resulting original collection of icons was exhibited for no more than a week at Kartell's Milan flagship store, before becoming the subject of a unique charity auction. Proceeds from the sale were donated to the Umberto Veronesi Foundation, which supports scientific research and cancer treatment.

Photography: Kartell

1

1
Missoni
Duomo 1992, 2011

2
AC Milan
Milan 25, 2011

2

3
Moschino
Madunina, 2011

4
Robert Wilson
**From Milano with Love,
2011**

5
Accademia
di Brera
**50 e 2 1/2 - Poesia e
Colore per Milano, 2011**

4

3

5

1

1
Ilovedust for Choice Cuts
DCW Eames Chair, 2009

Made by the Eames couple in 1946, the DCW Chair has survived over half a century as an icon of modern design. Inspired by a love of all things Eames, the designers of Ilovedust reinterpreted two LCW Eames chairs for Choice Cuts. The design was inspired by a dialogue between Charles and Ray Eames during the unveiling of the Eames Chair at the Arlene Francis Home Show. Ilovedust reworked quotes from the dialogue and interlocked them with 1950s style graphics. Each narrative pattern was applied onto the DCW Chair by hand. A series of limited edition cushions in green and blue were created as a supplement to the chair.

2
House Industries for Herman Miller
Typographic Eames Wire Base Tables, 2011

Herman Miller Asia-Pacific allied with House Industries to combine the classic Eames wire-base table with timeless typographic forms. Each tabletop is hand-printed at the House Industries Michigan factory and then returned to Herman Miller for assembly, where it is packaged in wooden crates specially designed by House Industries. The packing crates can later do double duty as storage containers. A limited-edition series of 80 tables includes the letters A through Z, numbers, and ornaments, all taken from from the House Industries Eames Century Modern font collection that culminated from a ten-year research and design partnership with the estate of Charles and Ray Eames.

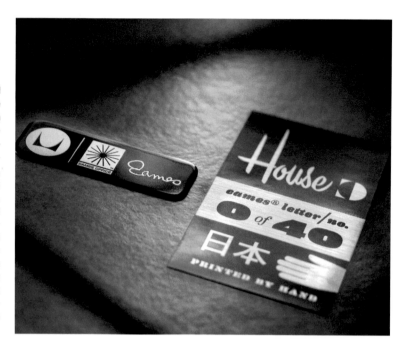

2

David Lynch
Silencio Cultural Night Club, 2011

Opening its doors on the Paris street of Rue Montmartre in August 2011, Silencio was the realization of David Lynch's vision for a unique club experience.

All furniture, textures, and materials were made to measure for the club, imagined and conceived by the famous filmmaker, who worked in close collaboration with Paris-based multidisciplinary Israeli designer Raphaël Navot. Architectural agency ENIA and a range of prestigious artists and designers pushed the limits of their savoir-faire by developing innovative materials to bring Lynch's original ideas to life.

The Silencio project is a cultural club dedicated to the creative community. Open from 6:00 pm to 6:00 am, it includes a movie theater of 24 seats, an intimate art library, a live stage, and a smoking room.

Photography: Alexandre Guirkinger/Silencio
Lightning: Thierry Dreyfus · Gold wood decor:
Les Ateliers Gohard · Movie theater: Quinette
· Manufacturer of furniture designed by David
Lynch in collaboration with Raphaël Navot ·
Domeau&Pérès · www.silencio-club.com

1
Domeau & Pérès for David Lynch's Silencio
Wire Chair, 2011

On the occasion of the opening of David Lynch's Paris night club Silencio, French furniture designers Bruno Domeau, a trained saddler, and Philippe Pérès, a trained upholsterer, collaborated with the famous director to create the Wire Chair. Designed for the club's library lounge, the curved metal structure is positioned under comfortable foam and fabric seats. The chairs were produced in a limited edition of 25, alongside the Blackbirds, a series of asymmetric, dynamic, faceted black leather seats and tables for the club's main space.

Photography: Sabine Pigalle

1

2

Kartell × Robert Wilson
7 Electric chairs... As you like it, 2011

The famous American director, stage designer and master of visual experimentation Robert Wilson has created a series of seven extraordinary luminous chair sculptures together with the Italian furniture makers at Kartell.

Premiering at the Teatro alla Scala in Milan in celebration of Wilson's 70th birthday, "7 Electric chairs... As you like it" draws inspiration from William Shakespeare's comedy As You Like It, particularly the celebrated monologue of the melancholy Jacques who speaks about the seven ages of man. Seven signifies not only the seven decades of Wilson's life, but also the seven extraordinary "thrones of light" which were be presented in their world premier at the Teatro alla Scala di Milano on the occasion of the premier of Wilson's staging of Claudio Monteverdi's opera, Il Ritorno di Ulisse in Patria. Bringing together two of his signature elements, chairs and light, Wilson, who in the course of his extraordinary career creates sculptures, drawings and furniture designs in addition to his stage work, created a collection of seven chairs, all of similar size but different in shape and made of transparent polycarbonate. This material, more than any other, characterizes the Kartell design brand. Seven series of seven assembled and hand-etched pieces were produced by Kartell to be sold to collectors by art galleries around the world.

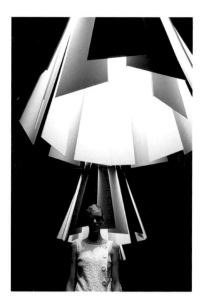

Tim Van Steenbergen for Delta Light
Metronome, 2011

Sharing a passion for creativity, timeless design, and craftsmanship, Delta Light joined forces with Belgian Fashion designer Tim Van Steenbergen to create a sculptural lamp shade. The result is the Metronome, a piece of pure and to-the-point dynamic lighting design influenced by catwalk drapery. The interesting layered construction conducts light into a magical play of shadows.

Launched in AMUZ, an international music center in a former monastery church in Antwerp, the Metronome was presented as part of a unique light installation. Five XXL versions of the pendant lamp provided an impressive piece of décor above Tim Van Steenbergen's 2012 summer collection catwalk show.

Photography: Tomas Vandecasteele

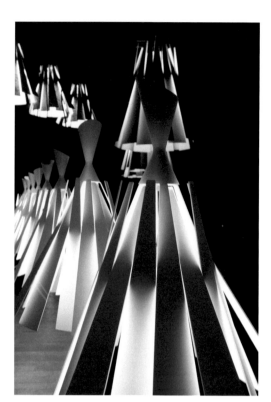

BLANQ for
Levi's x Fubon Art
Persona, 2011

Commissioned by Levi's and the Taiwanese Art Foundation Fubon Art, BLANQ turned recycled denim jeans into curious pieces of art. Staying true to Levi's "raw" personality, Jeffrey Wang and his team created a series of wearable denim sculptures. Held togeth- er by nothing but safety pins, the intricate pieces can be taken apart and worn again—a true recyclable project.

Studio Job and Viktor & Rolf have been friends for quite a while, and a particularly memorable time that the creative paths of the two duos crossed was on the occasion of the Credit Crunch Couture, the launch presentation of Viktor & Rolf's Spring/Summer 2010 Collection in Paris.

The Dutch fashion icons entrusted Studio Job with creating the scenography and objects for a show that would be performed by British singer Roisin Murphy at the event.

2

Core pieces of the extraordinary, surreal set included a spinning globe 175 centimeters in diameter and jeweled with 500,000 Swarovski crystals, a piece that the Dutch-Belgian duo had designed a year earlier as part of the Swarovski Pedestal collection.

Photography: P. Stigter[1], G. White[2]
Performer: Roisin Murphy[1]

75

PandaPanther x Amsterdam
Worldwide for Asics
Zodiac Race Shoe, 2009

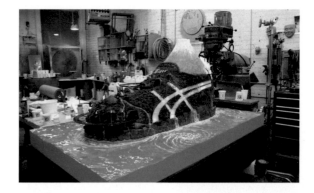

On the occasion of Onitsuka Tiger's 60th birthday, and under the creative direction of the international communications agency Amsterdam Worldwide, the designers of PandaPanther created a unique sculpture celebrating the brand's heritage.

In Japanese culture, the 60th birthday is a milestone of major significance laden with symbolism around the cycle of life concept, which is itself based on the Japanese zodiac calendar. Inspired by the shape and geological qualities of Japan, PandaPanther created a meter-long sneaker diorama resembling the legendary race of animals competing to become part of the zodiac calendar.

Apart from the sneaker island itself, the campaign was divulged across multiple communications channels, including an animation, print advertisements, online, and in stores.

Ogura Tansu Ten × Amsterdam Worldwide for Asics
Made of Japan Tansu, 2011

Banking on the Onitsuka Tiger heritage image and the brand's unique Japanese credentials, Asics—under Amsterdam Worldwide's creative direction—teamed up with the established cabinetry Ogura Tansu Ten to create the

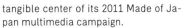

tangible center of its 2011 Made of Japan multimedia campaign.

Manufactured from authentic Paulownia wood in a four-month-long manual working process, the Ogura Tansu Ten sneaker sculpture reinterprets an old craft for a new generation, standing out against the digital noise

of today's media world and allaying the customer's growing thirst for authenticity.

Just like traditional tansu chests, the unique sneaker piece consists of a multitude of drawers, trays and hidden compartments, each of which harbors a precious little secret.

In Asic's flagship stores and in trade fairs worldwide, the handcrafted shoe intrigued fans with branded content, exclusive surprises, and safe deposits.

Packages with keys were sent to bloggers, allowing them exclusive access to certain compartments, generating buzz as they shared their discoveries online.

As a web version, over 1,200 stills created a fully interactive "virtual sneaker," revealing new collections, films, and surprise content.

PP. 78–79 | 1
Pinel & Pinel × Martell
Martell Cognac Trunk, 2011

Partnering with the House of Martell, the creative trunk-makers at Pinel & Pinel created a setting where cognac is the star. True to the love of fine craftsmanship and meticulous attention to detail, Pinel & Pinel designed the largest mobile trunk case ever produced: 2.06 meters high, 2.2 meters wide, and 0.7 meters deep. Made of precious materials such as full-grain leathers, copper, silver plate, oak, crystal, and linen, the brightly-lit Martell Trunk pays tribute to the art of cognac—to skill, quality, and patience. Ten craftsmen built, assembled, fashioned, and fitted the piece for a total of almost a thousand hours of labor.

2
Pinel & Pinel × Krug
Krug Picnic Trunk, 2005

Prestigious champagne-maker Krug selected Pinel & Pinel to create an exclusive picnic trunk dedicated to the eccentric picnic lover. An array of luxurious utensils conveys the art of nomad tableware. Included are a set of 10 specialized custom-made drawers, three niches for bottles plus one for the ice bucket, a self-assembling table made of the trunk's door, and four nickel legs. The piece, whose wooden structure is entirely coated in leather, was handmade by Pinel & Pinel's craftsmen in their Parisian workshop.

1

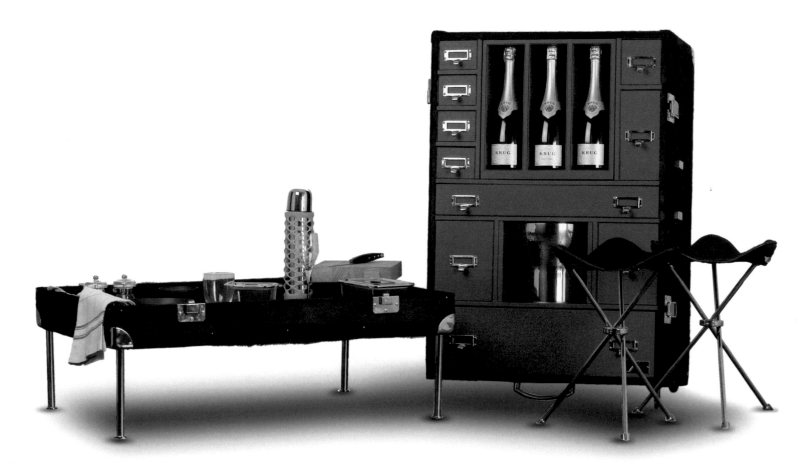

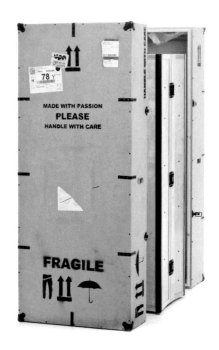
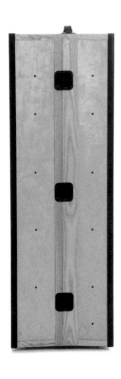
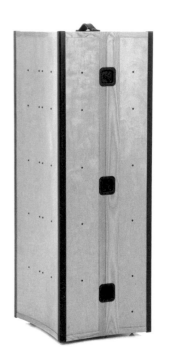

1

1
Method Furniture
× Denham the Jeanmaker
The Journeyman, 2011

Drawing inspiration from birch-bark canoes and bi-plane wing construction, Method Furniture created The Journeyman in collaboration with Denham the Jeanmaker. The modern interpretation of the classic steamer trunk has a solid ash frame, skinned with lightweight birch and hand-stitched leather. An uncompromising fusion of traditional and contemporary influences and techniques, the Journeyman boasts an array of custom detailing. The inward curving form allows only the outward edges, protected by locally hand-stitched leather, to touch the ground. Thick hand-cut leather handles, locked with beautifully-contrasting industrial case fittings allow for the trunk to be moved wherever it needs to go. Internally, the Journeyman contains a generous garment hanging space, sealed from the

elements by a handcrafted flysheet of the finest Japanese salvaged denim, detailed with re-cut vintage leather. Unlocking the hand-carved work surface reveals a column of carousels all carved from the same piece of solid ash, containing the tools of the jean maker's trade, such as spare buttons, rivets, and thread spools.

2
Goyard × Assouline
Leather Trunks, 2010 – ongoing

Famous French high-end luggage maker Goyard teamed up with New York-based luxury publisher Assouline to create a very special trunk. Custom-made for affluent bibliophile globetrotters, each trunk houses 100 of Assouline's signature memoir photobiographies on art, fashion, design and architecture. An ongoing project, both black and white versions of the trunks

are still available at international Assouline Boutiques. Their suggested retail price is $20,000.

2

Jean Paul Gaultier for Roche Bobois
Anniversary Collection, 2010

French furniture design house Roche Bobois invited Jean Paul Gaultier to create a series of furniture pieces to commemorate the brand's 50th anniversary. The result is a bold and energetic collection that celebrates the close kinship between fashion and interior design, and the key elements that both disciplines share: creativity, aesthetics, expertise, and a loving attention to detail. Along these lines, the transformable, mahjong-like pieces manifest the unique imagination of the French fashion designer combined with Roche Bobois' expertise.

The Anniversary Collection includes a bedroom set, a sofa, armchairs, and a range of complementary accessories, all in typical Gaultier prints, including his signature nautical stripes. Some of the particularly exclusive pieces formed part of a limited-edition series of 250 pieces.

Photography: Michel Gibert

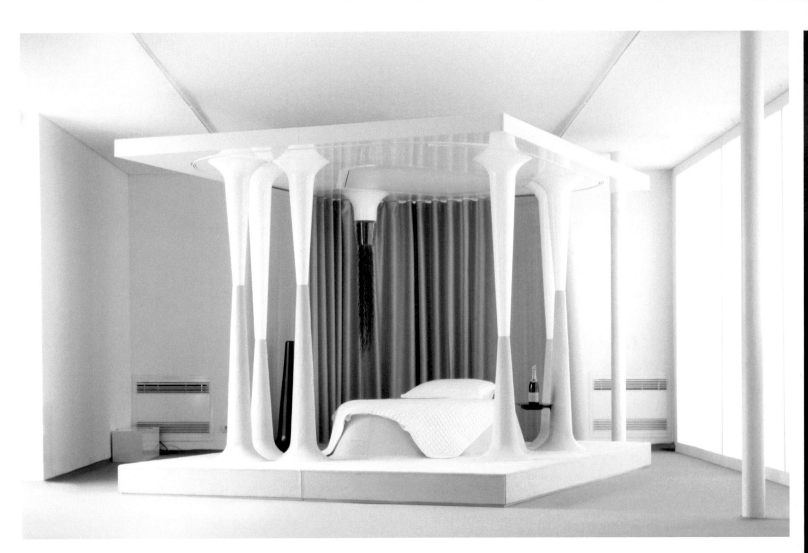

Mathieu Lehanneur for Veuve Clicquot
Once Upon a Dream Installation, 2010

Veuve Clicquot's partnerships are the fruit of a deep-seated commitment. Since Barbe-Nicole Clicquot Ponsardin created the very first riddling table in 1816, innovation has been at the heart of the company's calling. The company's association with Mathieu Lehanneur is linked to the renovation of Veuve Clicquot's Reims town house, the Hôtel du Marc, which is said to embody the essence of Madame Clicquot's spirit. To represent the Hôtel du Marc's vocation of welcome, aesthetics, and pleasure, Lehanneur presented the installation Once Upon a Dream, a high-tech sleeping unit for jet-lagged Veuve Clicquot house guests. Designed on the basis of medical data gathered by a sleep specialist, the project harkens back to Madame Clicquot, who suffered from chronic insomnia—and thus to the very beginning of Veuve Clicquot history.

Mathieu Lehanneur's project was previewed at the 2011 Milan Furniture Fair, alongside commissioned pieces by the Brazilian designers Fernando & Humberto Campana.

Photography: Thomas Duval

Front Design for Veuve Clicquot
Chaise Lounge, 2009

Inspired by the DesignBox, Veuve Clicquot's exclusive eco-friendly gift package, Stockholm-based creative collective Front Design developed the chaise lounge, a seat built of Veuve Clicquot champagne boxes. The pile of boxes has a hidden center of foam, which makes the seemingly-uncomfortable chaise lounge a surprisingly soft piece of furniture to sit on. Randomly positioned, the boxes create a pixelated effect.

The project is part of a series of three collaborations initiated under the umbrella concept "Out of the Box," an initiative born from Veuve Clicquot's determination to break free from the functional constraints associated with the production of the new DesignBox and its industrialization. In this context, the Chaise Lounge was released at Milan Furniture Fair 2009, alongside designs by Tom Dixon and 5.5 Designers.

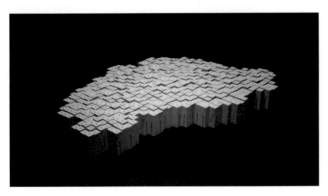

5.5 Designers for Veuve Clicquot
Champagne Cellar, 2009

Veuve Clicquot harnessed the provocative side of 5.5 Designers for a collaborative project. The result of the collaboration is a sculptural storage unit that offers the ability to savor Clicquot's Yellow Label champagne. Drawing inspiration from construction brick according to the tradition of old champagne cellar walls, the Paris-based design team plunged into an atmosphere that is 100% Veuve Clicquot. Taking cues from both architecture and furniture design, 5.5 Designers developed new typologies to equip the brand with a unique, flexible solution for storage and presentation.

Based on the story summed up as, "from the brick to the building," the installation can be broken down into four elements: first, there are the individual bricks, each containing one bottle of champagne to be stacked inside the Veuve Clicquot case-drawer. Second, the bucket, a cooler-to-go, is designed as a synthesis between a traditional champagne bucket and the Veuve Clicquot case-drawer. Third is the stool (or bench, when put together), built on the base of four champagne bottles stacked in their cases, for one to sit upon and enjoy a glass of champagne. And, last but not least, the Wall of Champagne is the sum of the furniture and walls perceived in their entity, including a table jutting out from amidst the case structure to provide a storage space for bottles.

The project was introduced at Milan Furniture Fair 2009 as part of the Veuve Clicquot "Out of the Box" initiative, a series of collaborations based on a creative interpretation of champagne casing.

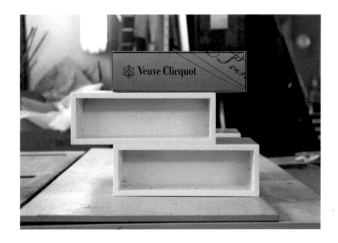

Tom Dixon for
Veuve Clicquot
Comet Lamp, 2009

Using the Veuve Clicquot DesignBox as a starting point, British designer Tom Dixon focused on the complexities of engineering a simple-looking cardboard object. Fascinated by the beauty of basic shapes and geometry as a key concept of design, Dixon researched Veuve Clicquot's mysterious six-pointed star logo, discovering references to an auspicious comet seen in the night skies of the Champagne region of France in 1811. Inspired by the infinite possibilities of translating this reference into three-dimensions, Dixon envisioned what became the Comet Lamp and installation, which are as "romantic and sparkling" as champagne.

A limited edition of 500 Comet Lamps was produced and presented as part of Veuve Clicquot's "Out of the Box" initiative at Milan Furniture Fair 2009, on the occassion of the launch of the new DesignBox.

Performance

Staging Brands—
Shows of Seduction and Strategy

The brand-visibility concepts in the following section are prime examples of corporate communication made to astonish.

Some amaze us with marvelous displays, a sense of wonder, and narrative structure, such as Nendo's PP. 146–147 retrospective for Akio Hirata, and Visual Editions's PP. 112–113 window installation at Vitsœ's London store. Some dazzle us with wit, like Frank Anselmo's

1

PP. 132–133 What Goes Around Comes Around posters, commissioned by the Global Coalition For Peace. Other projects catch us by surprise, occurring unexpectedly in unconventional locations—or even shock us, such as the Magician's Trunk that David & Goliath P. 127 developed to promote Lance Burton's performance at MGM Resorts. Again others, like Trigger Happy Production's PP. 140–143 House of Imagination, made for the German home improvement store Hornbach, pique our curiosity, since we need to look closer in order to discover the brand association.

Stimulating interest is inextricably tied to brands' commercial interests, but there is room for much else to happen along the way. Many projects in the following section blur the border between branding and art. Sometimes they tear down the distinction altogether—not only due to their appeal as sculptures or installations, but often because they are conceived of and implemented by individuals renowned in the international art world.

Alliances of this kind are not a new phenomenon. In the 1930s, well-known surrealists like Salvador Dalí and Marcel Duchamp created stage-ready backdrops and spectacular branded scenery for commercial displays. In the 1950s, Robert Rauschenberg and Jasper Johns started their careers trimming shop windows. Particularly in New York, fabricating large department store displays has long been considered an effective creative outlet, allowing artists to present their work to the masses and make money at the same time. The high degree of creative innovation that these opportunities allow has practically turned some metropolitan shopping districts into admission-free, around-the-clock art galleries, infusing everyday life with moments of fine art.

Today, the celebrated retail spaces of flagship stores and trade fairs seem to host the most elaborate occurrences of corporate performance. Here, retail spaces overlap with the realm of visual merchandising, a particular field of marketing in which brands frequently commission artists and architects. For instance, Prada had its stores designed by the Dutch architect and Jack-of-all-design-trades Rem Koolhaas. Italian luxury leather goods company Fendi entrusted a group of students of Royal College of Art to create in-store performances and installations for the opening of its London flagship boutique. Other performance-based

2

brand projects occur in locations that are rather unexpected and often public, yet always carefully selected. They are usually part of greater campaigns, and range from outdoor billboards to interactive installations.

Whether these endeavors are classified as visual merchandising or advertising, every example of exceptional corporate performance is a precarious undertaking for a brand to attempt. A branded piece of art might be interpreted as pretentious, or viewed as too gaudy and imposing. Particularly far out examples of unconventional advertising run the risk of being considered an unwelcome intrusion into public space. Furthermore, it my be hard to sell the concepts internally within the company; many of these experiments do not follow long-established marketing rules and discourage direct evaluation of profit potential, as their effectiveness can often only be judged by the buzz they create. Unorthodox strategies demand confidence and a strong belief in the wow-factor they might eventually achieve.

In the case of projects involving an artist, this person also runs a risk. After all, commercial commissions always entail delicate negotiations and compromises. When Dalí designed windows for the New York fashion boutique Bonwit Teller & Co., his work was deemed as promotional and shallow by many of his fellow artists. Critical voices of his time raised concerns over art's integration into capitalist culture, reducing the artist's role to no more than a shop designer. However, by the time Andy Warhol began his career decorating shop windows, this concern was already less of a problematic issue.

Many contemporary examples illustrate the ways in which commercial commissions can be considered experimental platforms that encourage and nurture creatives from various artistic fields. Then again, a range of commercial decorators like Simon Doonan, who is the creative director at the New York-based department store Barneys, are celebrated as art icons rather than simply commercial craftsmen. Indeed, Doonan's his work is artistically sophisticated, conceptual, and bursting with creative innovation. In other words, corporate commissions do not necessarily lead to corporate interference or a dampening of artistic potential.

From the brand perspective, artistic corporate performance can work wonders, and can achieve highly sought-after cultural credibility. In order for this to happen, the brand must believe in the project and the artist it chooses to work with. Of course, brands want to market themselves well, so their ultimate objective is certainly to attract, engage, and motivate the customer to make a purchase. Many brands understand that this implies creating something new and exciting, and thus give artists a free hand. The artist's creative toolkit may include color, lighting, space, and sensory inputs such as smell, touch, and sound—as well as groundbreaking technological systems and interactive installations.

Developed and implemented with a great deal of care and energy, and often requiring a great deal of collaboration due to the projects' complexity, which often calls for specific expertise, the examples at hand in the following section are rarely designed to stand the test of time. Some ventures perish on the the very same day that they are created, like Trigger Happy Production's P. 144 snowmen on strike for Entega, or endure only a couple of weeks, to be marveled at by those who get the news, spread the message, or are lucky enough to be in the right place at the right time.

In their transitory nature, the projects in this section embody the very spirit of our time, with today's short-lived trends and fleeting information. As to their outstanding creative visions, they counter the equalizing tendency of the global mass market. Their core values, however, lie in their orchestration, in the often wisely-staged experiences that endure in the public imagination, making all of us wish we had seen them ourselves.

1 | PP. 112 – 113
InkValley for
Visual Editions × Vitsœ
Visual Editions at Vitsœ, 2011/2012

Installation by InkValley-London × Art Direction: Elke Hanspach × Set Design: Sabrina Lee Hammon × Photography: Ryan Hopkinson

2 | PP. 94 – 95
Gerry Judah for
Goodwood Festival of Speed
Car Sculptures, 1997-2012

Photography: David Barbour

Gerry Judah for Goodwood Festival of Speed

Car Sculptures, 1997–2012

Gerry Judah produced his car-themed installations for the Goodwood Festival of Speed, a celebration of classic cars and racing held annually in the English county of Sussex. Since 1997, he has astonished the festival's visitors with sculptures of enormous scale. The Jaguar E-Type piece, for example, consists of half a kilometer of a steel tube 1200-millimeters in diameter, which stands 28 meters tall and weighs over 175 kilos, aiming to embody the spirit of the world's leading automakers. Judah's project has involved stringing up Ferraris, affixing Range Rovers and Audis to giant metal structures, and forming giant Alfa red lines of steel to twist into the air—just to mention some examples.

Photography: David Barbour

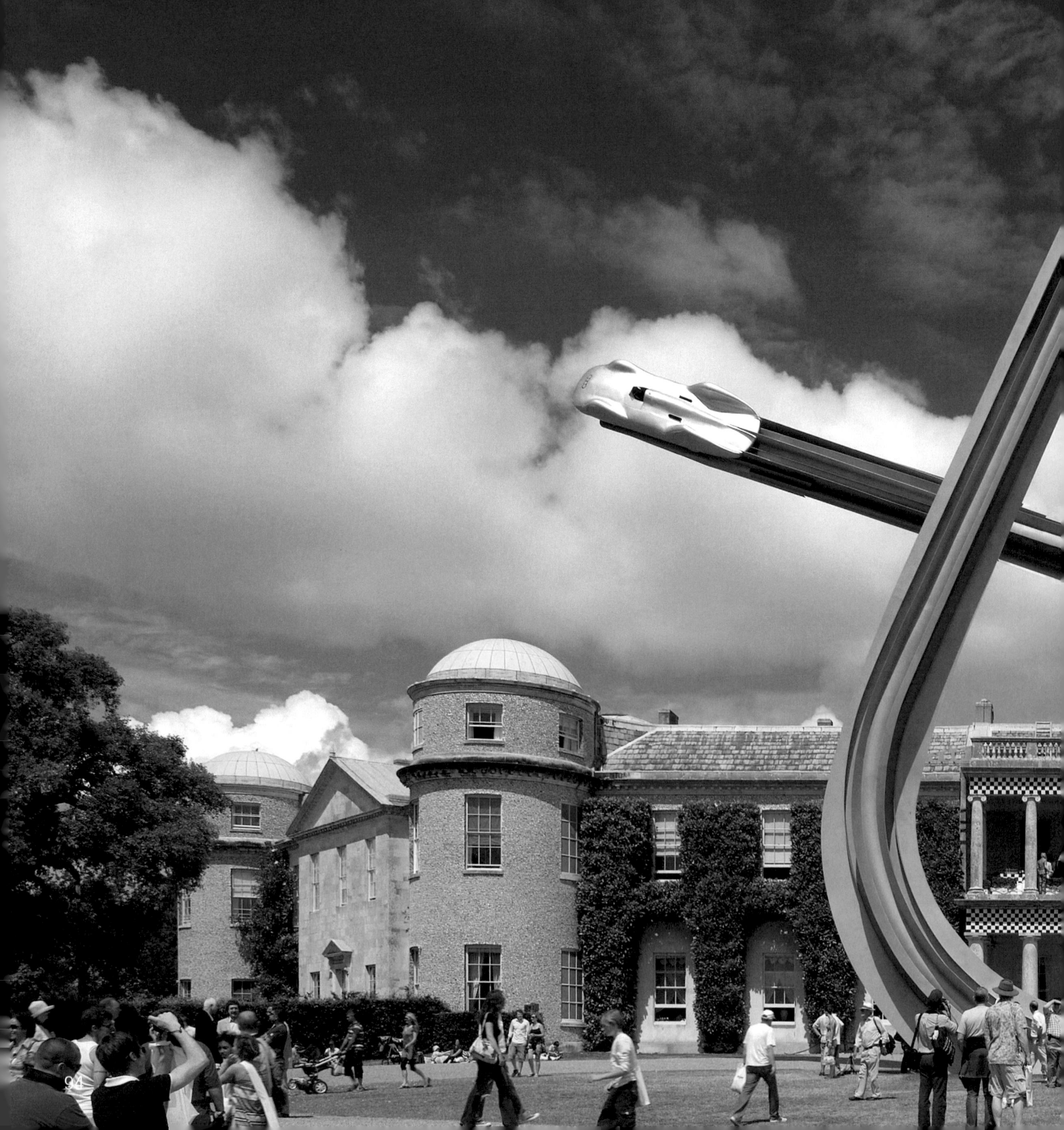

Sarah Illenberger
× K-MB Berlin
× CARTONDRUCK for Smart
Camousmart, 2010

Sarah Illenberger collaborated with the Berlin-based brand agency K-MB and the creative packaging company CARTONDRUCK to camouflage the Smart Fortwo car with thousands of little cardboard boxes. In keeping with the car's eco-friendly image, they used recyclable paper from the traditional German paper manufactory Gmund in a variety of different shades of green.

Photography: © Daimler AG

Amigos del Museo de Arte Popular
Vochol, 2010

The Vochol project is an homage to the artistic traditions and skills of the Huichol people, a Native American ethnic group of western central Mexico living in the Sierra Madre Occidental range.

The collaboration of the Museum of Popular Art and the Association of Friends of the Museum of Popular Art (AAMAP) was supported by the governments of the Huichol's home states of Jalisco and Nayarit, and realized with the help of eight Huichol artists who devoted more than nine thousand hours of their time to transferring their inspiration to a magical, colorful design of about 90 kilograms of glass seed beads embedded onto a Volkswagen.

A broad program of promotional activities publicizing the Vochol throughout 2011 culminated in the car's international sale, with all proceeds donated to the AAMAP, allowing the association to continue upholding its objective of safeguarding and promoting the work of more than eight million Mexican artisans.

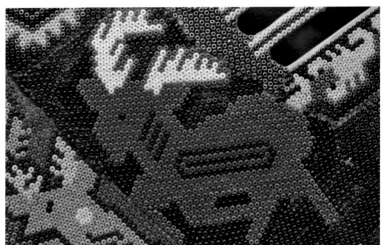

Fabio Novembre for
Fiat × The City of Milan
Per Fare un Albero, 2009

Trusting that trees, not supernatural
beings with wings, are our real guard-
ian angels, Italian architect and interi-
or designer Fabio Novembre developed
a good-humored campaign to promote
the idea of public greening, along with
the city of Milan and automaker Fiat. Per
Fare un Albero ("Create a Tree") unites
trees and motorcars, which otherwise
tend to compete for space in the urban landscape, to become partners in a
peaceful demonstration lining the road-
side of Milan's Via Montenapoleone.
The temporary installation features 20
fiberglass Fiat 500C replicas as planters
for different types of trees, and demonstrates both Fiat's and the municipali-
ty's commitment to making the city of
Milan more livable.

Photography: Giuseppe Modeo

ART+COM for BMW Museum
Kinetic Sculpture, 2008

ART+COM was commissioned to design all media elements and interactive installations in the new BMW museum in Munich, which opened in 2008. A part of this challenge was to create a spatial installation that communicated the design process of a vehicle in a metaphorical and poetic manner. The installation needed to set the tone for the entire exhibition, attuning visitors to the museum from the very beginning by taking center stage in the "Inspiration" room, in the museum's House of Design. BMW devoted the first station of the exhibition tour to one of the central thematic focuses of the museum: the interplay of mechanical and electronic components creates a dynamic art piece, representing the museum of mobility in the most literal sense. A levitating surface that consists of 714 metal spheres, hanging from thin steel wires attached to individually-controlled stepper motors, enabled the orchestration of complex three-dimensional shape animations in free space and mirrored the precise interplay between many single elements from which one coherent picture emerged. At the beginning of the seven-minute choreography, all spheres move chaotically, and then, from the cloud of spheres depicting indefinite ideas, several competing blueprints gradually resolve into a final shape. The shape that forms suggests the outlines of well-known BMW automobiles such as the 327, the 1500, the Z4 coupé and the Mille Miglia 2006 Concept Car. Audio quotes from BMW designers and engineers about the company's values and design aims accompany the narration.

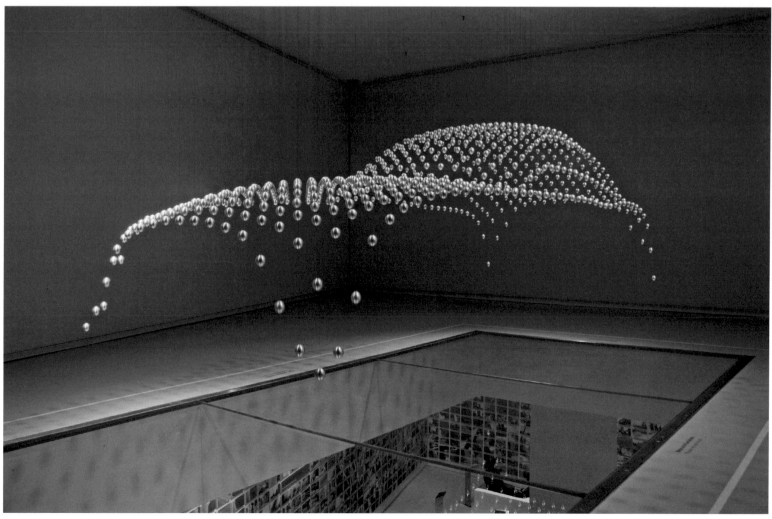

Omer Arbel for Bocci
28 Garage Installation, 2011

Taking advantage of Omer Arbel's glassblowing abilities, Canadian design collective Bocci deviated slightly from their otherwise extremely functional style to present a series of sculptural chandeliers. Arbel experimented with sand-casting and glassblowing techniques and came up with a range of unconventional pieces.

Omer Arbel's installation at the No-Ho Design District presented 28 of his chandeliers hung 15 meters high in a New York City garage, conveying a phenomenological impression of the city landscape.

Photography: Gwenael Lewis

103

Arnaud Lapierre for Audi
The Ring Installation, 2011

The Ring is Arnaud Lapierre's creative interpretation of Audi's core values: dynamics and experience. Inviting the visitor to come in and become part of an environment of perpetual flux, the installation is based on the constantly-shifting relationship between individuals and the space that surrounds them. Inspired by urban networks and their complex interactivity, The Ring visualizes rhythm, flow, and the notions of spatial organization and hierarchy. The arrangement of cubic mirrors fractures typical spatial perception, while at the same time connecting all its elements through multiple reflections.

The Ring was installed on the occasion of the FIAC art fair in Paris, where it could be visited at Place Vendôme.

Photography: Eric Mercier, Arnaud Lapierre

A.F. VANDEVORST
Aktion I – IV, 2009 – 2011

Since the foundation of the label in the late 1990s, A.F. Vandevorst has undertaken a range of outside design projects and collaborations. The label's Aktionen project is its traveling guerilla store that shows and sells its collections in a quaint medical setting, complete with iron-framed hospital beds, utility weighing machines, drug cabinets, control screens, and staff dressed in clinical white with signature red armbands.

Playing on the Red Cross logo and the label's overall style, the Aktion project invites customers to experience the world and signature style of A.F. Vandevorst, but also to reinforce the brand's connection with the world of art as an area of reference. Building on the complimentary dynamic that art and fashion share, the project's four iterations were developed in close cooperation with artist collaborators and cultural organizations such as the Hoet Bekaert Gallery and the Museum Dr. Guslain in Ghent.

From 2009 to 2011, the Aktion guerilla store traveled to Antwerp, Knokke-Zoute, Ghent, and Knokke–Heist.

Photography: Ann Vallé

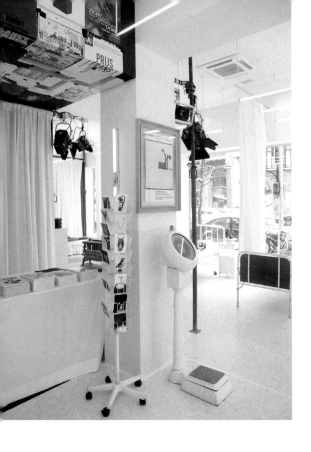

A.F. Vandevorst
× Hoet Bekaert Gallery
**The Smallest Travelling Store in the
World, 2010 (ongoing)**

An extension of the Aktionen traveling guerilla store project, A.F. Vandevorst's traveling store is a "shop-in-a-shop" installation, bringing together visual elements and materials of reference that illustrate the concept behind the A.F. Vandevorst label, as well as the brand's spiritual kinship with the world of art.

Resembling a patient's hospital room, the installation picks up on the medical theme of the larger guerilla store project, reinforcing it as an important source of inspiration. The artistic interpretation of A.F. Vandevorst's fashion becomes a performance, staged to let the customer experience an extraction of the brand's unique atmosphere.

After being shown at London's Dover Street Market in September 2010, the installation traveled to Dutch Design Week in Eindhoven in October 2010, then to Selfridges in London, and then to the Arnhem Mode Biennale in Summer 2011, settling down for any length of time at A.F. Vandevorst retailer Jones Arnhem.

Photography: Ann Vallé

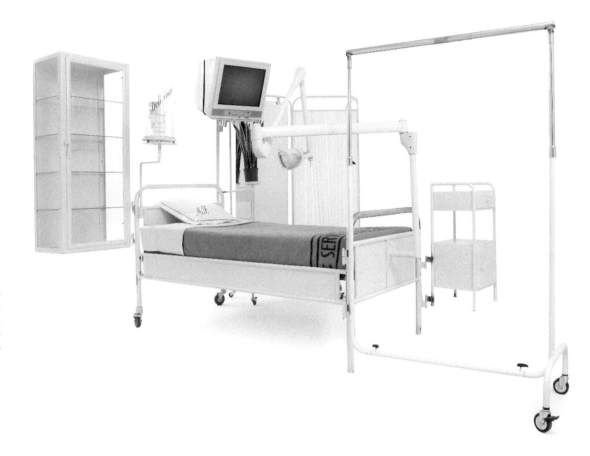

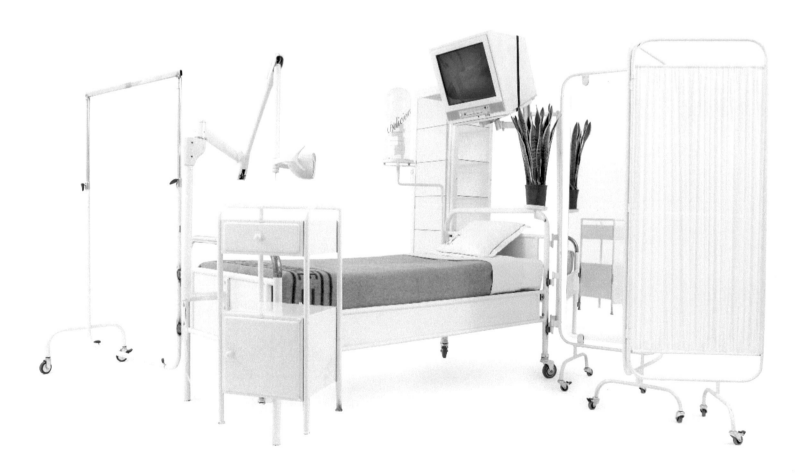

109

Aether Apparel
× Thierry Gaugain
AetherStream, 2011

Aether Apparel teamed up with Paris-based designer Thierry Gaugain to create the ultimate shop on wheels. From the very beginning, the Aether team had its eyes set on repurposing the classic Airstream PanAmerica. After finding the ultimate RV, a 10-meter toy hauler that has a rear hatch perfect for a store entrance, Jonah Smith and Palmer West of Aether completely gutted the interior and redesigned it from the floor up. They then searched the world for a designer who could translate their ideas and desires into a design concept, finally finding Thierry Gaugain, a designer who understood what they were trying to accomplish.

Gaugain spent the following 15 years working side-by-side with Philippe Starck in order to design a multitude of interior spaces, appliances,

motorcycles, and yachts, launching his own international studio in 2011. Based on extensive experience and cross-disciplinary expertise, he managed to bring the Aether Apparel design project to life.

The flooring of the store is 11-inch reclaimed oak, made by Carlisle Wide Plank Floors. The shop's sofa and table were custom-made by Environment Furniture, a company that uses sustainable harvested wood and incorporates the reuse of otherwise discarded materials. Most props and other furniture were purchased at the Paris flea market.

Starting out in Los Angeles in 2011, the AetherStream toured the USA, bringing key pieces from the Aether fall 2011 collection directly to the customer.

Photography: Aether

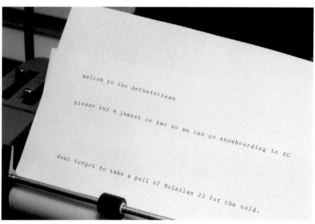

welcom to the Aetherstream

please buy a jacket or two so we can go snowboarding in BC

dont forget to take a pull of McCallan 25 for the cold.

VITSŒ

Magpie Studio for
Gavin Martin Colournet
Proof Bags, 2010

Looking to raise their profile within the design industry, the award-winning printers at Gavin Martin Colournet commissioned London-based Magpie Studio to develop a particularly striking packaging solution. Realizing that the bags they use to deliver proofs presented an untapped opportunity as a mobile advertising canvas, they asked the designers to brand these bags in

a way that would be eye-catching and memorable. Magpie Studio's solution is an interactive one; a fun and seemingly random collection of hand-delivered objects were screen-printed onto cardboard bags, raising a smile and spurring conversation every time their proofs are dropped off or picked up.

UbachsWisbrun/JWT
for Mini Cooper
Mini Christmas Box Campaign, 2009

Looking for an appropriate closing offensive for its "99 Euro" campaign, Mini Cooper had Amsterdam-based advertising agency UbachsWisbrun/JWT create Mini Christmas Boxes. Seizing upon the familiar day-after-Christmas street scene, the creatives placed over-sized cardboard containers amongst all the rubbish bags, thrown out Christmas trees, and gift packaging. The 99-Euro price tag affixed to each box took the story of the car as an affordable Christmas present to extremes and—whether or not the price was convincing—the idea certainly spread like wildfire.

FOAM for Dry the River
3D Paper-Craft Poster Project, 2011

To promote the new signing of London-based band Dry the River, RCA Records commissioned the advertising agency FOAM to create an unconventional poster campaign. The result of this request was the creation of huge 3D horses leaping out of the posters, which FOAM intern Xavier Barrade developed in Google SketchUp. All the components of his design were printed and assembled by hand; each poster took around 35 hours to complete. Pasted up around London, the posters achieved great coverage in the art, design, creative, and music press, and caused Dry the River's official video to rocket from 10,000 views to over 300,000 views.

Designers: Xavier Barrade, Phil Clandillon, Steve Milbourne   Executive Producer: Simon Poon Tip   Photography: Ricky Stanton Screen Printing: Bob Eight Pop

PP. 118–121
Sarah Illenberger
for MYKITA

Heads Up!, 2011

Berlin-based illustrator Sarah Illenberger created a series of sculptural
product displays for the up-and-coming
eyewear makers at MYKITA. Her series
of curious heads presented the brand's
designer spectacles in stores and shop
windows.

Photography: Ragnar Schmuck

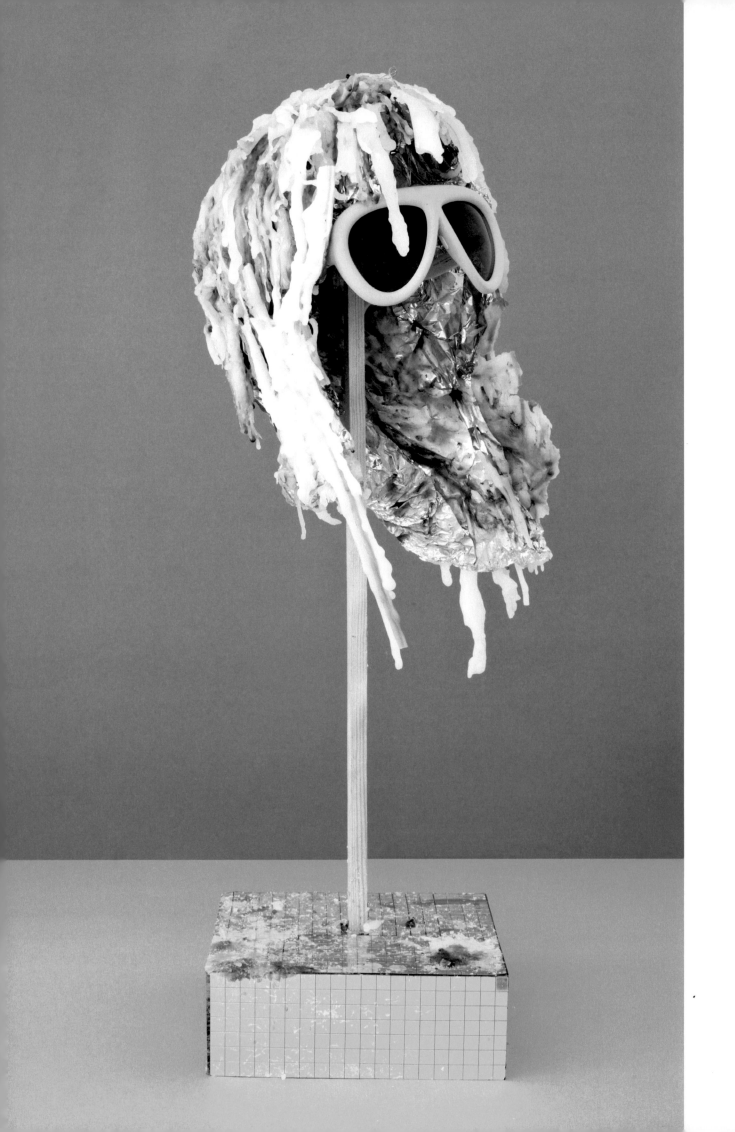

Pantone for
Basheer Graphic Books
Pantone Rainbow, 2009

Basheer Graphic Books commissioned Asian communications agency Bates to develop a marketing concept that would promote their Pantone color guide book to art college students, acquaint them with Pantone's extensive color selection, and give printing guidance. To grab the young target group's attention, the creatives at Bates set up a huge rainbow of more than 5,000 Pantone color chips, 8 meters long and 4.5 meters high. Installed in a college park for one month's time, the colorful spectacle introduced students to Pantone's real-life colors and caused Basheer Graphic Books' sales to increase significantly.

Creatives: Andreas Junus, Irawandhani Kamarga, Hendra Lesmono, Iyan Susanto, Bates Asia Jakarta   Photography: Handri Karya

Volt for
Norwegian Airlines
Parasols, 2011

The first colors of spring in Gothenburg in 2011 weren't flowers, but nearly 1000 small drink parasols. Put up by Stockholm-based advertising agency Volt in a variety of public places, they served as a reminder that summer had already arrived at many of Norwegian Airline's destinations in southern Europe. Every single parasol had a price tag quoting the airline's special offers for all those who felt like skipping spring and going straight to summer.

1

3

2

4

Byggstudio for Nike × Liberty × Monki
The Floriographic Garden, 2011

On the occassion of the Nike × Liberty sneaker collection release, Byggstudio created Floriographic Garden, a flower garden that was installed in Stockholm in May 2011. The project's overall theme was the language of flowers, or "floriography," a communication system whose meaning is based on different flower species, which was developed and used during the Victorian era in England. The Floriographic Garden's flower meadow contained various floriographic messages, basing its design on a creative reinterpretation of Liberty's classic flower patterns. An interactive booth allowed visitors to create fresh bouquets on-site, and typographic wrapping paper explained the meanings of the various flowers.

Expanding on the Floriographic Garden concept, Byggstudio created a "flower language meadow" for the opening party of the Monki Flagship Store in Stockholm, where guests were invited to pick a "personal message bouquet" from the meadow that the gardener, Maja, translated into flower language.

Photography: Hanna Nilsson [2 3],
Anna Lundh [1 4], Märta Thisner [5 6 7]

5

6

PICK YOUR OWN BUNCH
OF WORDS HERE

7

2

1
Sagmeister for Levi's
The Strongest Thread, 2008

When Levi Strauss & Co. asked Sagmeister Inc. to design a poster for Levi's classic 501 jeans, Sagmeister ended up creating a poster out of the jeans themselves. Deconstructed down to the individual threads and buttons, these raw materials were reformed to create an explanatory message: "This is a pair of Levi's, sewed with the strongest thread."

Creative Director: Stefan Sagmeister   Design: Joe Shouldice, Richard The   Photography: Tom Schierlitz   Director of Print Services: Meredith Ball   Production Company: MORE-media   Director: Josh Forbes   Production Designer: Bradd Wesley Fillmann   Media Consultant: GranDesign

1

2
David&Goliath for MGM Resorts International
Lance Burton Trunk Installation, 2010

Lance Burton is a master magician whose show celebrates the artistry and classic magic of the great illusionists. To promote his headlining show at Monte Carlo Resort and Casino, international creative agency David & Goliath played on an iconic and clas-sic illusion. Placing half of a trunk of the type used in the famous "lady sawn in half" illusion on airport baggage carousels, they managed to demonstrate the timeless mesmerizing effect of magic in Burton's performances.

Chief Creative Officer: David Angelo   Executive Creative Director: Colin Jeffery   Design Director: John Kieselhorst   Associate Creative Directors: Napper Tandy/David Cuccinello   Art Director: Bryan Carroll   Copywriter: Aroon Mukhey   Photography: Kate Montgomery

127

1

2

1
Frank Anselmo for School of Visual Arts
Think, 2008

Commissioned by the School of Visual Arts to promote its wide selection of creative programs, ad-man Frank Anselmo encouraged New York pedestrians to see the world from a different perspective. Huge loose-leaf notebook pages made of heavy-duty anti-slip vinyl were affixed on sidewalks beneath bicycle racks at a skewed angle, to remind pedestrians that the world is full of unexpected sources of inspiration.

Creatives: Jeseok Yi, Frank Anselmo/Agency: KNARF — Creative directors: Frank Anselmo, Richard Wilde — Photography: Billy Siegrist

2
Frank Anselmo for the Natural Resources Defense Council (NRDC)
Hot Cups and Protective Sleeves, 2007

To illustrate and communicate the problem of global warming on behalf of the Natural Resources Defense Council, Frank Anselmo created a set of hot cups and protective sleeves. The message is clear: if the world is a cup, the NRDC aims to act as its sleeve

Creatives: Kevin Honegger, Stephen Minasvand/Agency: KNARF — Executive creative director: Frank Anselmo — Photography: Billy Siegrist

3
Frank Anselmo for HBO
Arm and Cement Shoes, 2005

Assigned to create buzz for HBO's award-winning modern-day mafia series The Sopranos, New York-based creative director and founder of the School of Visual Arts' "Unconventional Advertising" program Frank Anselmo had some life-like arms made. The arms were formed using casts taken from real human arms and constructed from plastic. Fitted with suit jacket and silk shirt, cufflinks, and the traditional gold pinky ring indicative of an assassinated mafia hit man, the arms were affixed to the trunks of NYC Taxi cabs, creating the impression that an actual body was stuffed inside. A simple bumper sticker with The Sopranos logo was stuck beside the hand.

Creatives: Frank Anselmo, Jayson Atienza, Chris Maiorino/Agency: BBDO — Chief creative officer: David Lubars

3

Dorten × Peter Sutherland
for Axel Springer AG / Welt
Kompakt

Rastloser Planet (Restless Planet), 2011

Stuttgart-based creative agency
Dorten, who linked up with New York
artist Peter Sutherland to develop a
campaign based on unsettling im-

(Restless Planet) illustrate the way
in which an internet-driven generation utilizes a variety of different media sources, often simultaneously.
The underlying notion of the "restless
planet" was played out as an integrated communications campaign in diverse channels in parallel: As an outdoor poster, as print advertisements,
as an online campaign, and as cine-

ma and TV advertisements that played
with the principle of sampling by reus-
ing and rearranging found footage

Artist: Peter Sutherland × Agency: Dorten
GmbH × Photography: Manuel Wagner and
Landon Metz[1]

1

Germany's newest daily paper
aims to inspire a potential reader-
ship that, for the most part, doesn't
read printed newspapers any-
more. Welt Kompakt commissioned

age collages that address and engage internet-attuned target groups.
Referring to the method of "information sampling," Sutherland's eighteen
visuals entitled "Rastloser Planet"

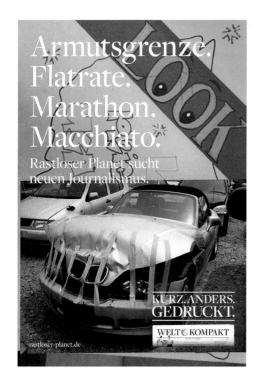

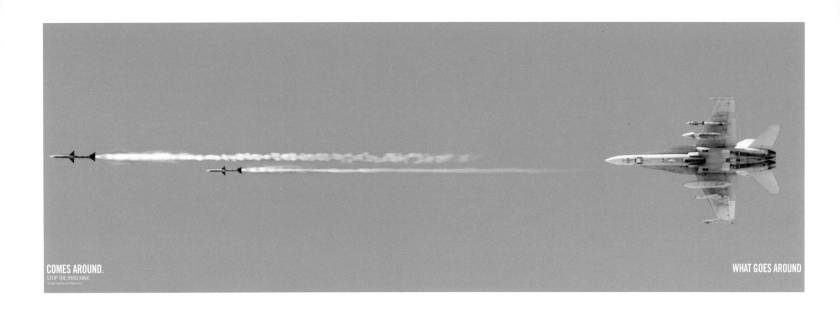

Frank Anselmo for
Global Coalition For Peace
What Goes Around Comes Around, 2010

This simple outdoor poster campaign focused on the spiraling cycle of war, reminding viewers that the violence perpetrated abroad will breed the hatred that fuels tomorrow's violence—What Goes Around Comes Around.

Creative directors: Frank Anselmo, Richard Wilde, Alfred S. Park

Sagmeister for Levi's
Levi's Billboard, 2010

Commissioned by Levi's Creative Director Len Peltier, Sagmeister Inc. focused on Levi Strauss & Co.'s workwear heritage to create an unconventional billboard. The sign's typography is positioned on turning cogwheels, and its kinetic panel is constantly breaking down and rebuilding itself—literally performing its message: "We are all workers." The piece was installed at the intersec-tion of Houston and Lafayette Streets in New York City's SoHo district.

Designer: Jessica Walsh · Production: Atomic Props

2 opposite page

lg2 for Festival de Magie de Québec
Magic Hat, 2011

Commissioned to promote the first edition of the Festival de Magie de Qué-bec, Luc Du Sault and Vincent Bernard of the Canadian advertising agency lg2 developed a truly memorable billboard. A mysteriously minimal ad space in the middle of Quebec City was coiffed by an immense top hat, as if by magic, from which pigeons emerged.

The installation was featured in a variety of local newspapers, radio pro-grams, and blog posts, and helped the festival achieve a successful debut.

Designers: Luc Du Sault and Vincent Bernard of lg2 · Account Manager : Sandie Lafleur, Eve Boucher

1, 2 opposite page

1

2

There may be parallels between the world of advertising and gunfights, but Trigger Happy Productions doesn't shoot from the hip. In the crossfire of communication, the Berlin-based multi-media production company follows a sensible strategy, which appears to respond particularly well to the changing requirements of contemporary brand communication.

Founded in 1996 by photographer and director Ralf Schmerberg along with producer Eva Maier-Schönung, Trigger Happy Productions produces a wide range of media including commercials, feature films, documentaries, viral shorts and animations. The film and TV projects they produce as a full service agency connect with the audience through contemporary storytelling. The brand communication strategies they develop act on the principle that people don't want to be told stories, but to become part of them.

With the The House of Imagination, a local campaign they developed for the German home improvement store Hornbach, or the thought-provoking "Denkanstöße," a series of promotional

the jaded consumer in an engaging, stimulating way and become the topics of lively conversation. Word of mouth plays an important role in this strategy. But rather than putting too much energy into trying to manipulate a viral effect, Trigger Happy Productions works by instinct in the hopes of simply creating projects that are worth talking about.

"Our main goal is to bring all different kinds of people together to create interesting projects. We don't care too much about the wow-effect, and we believe that you're more likely to get a 'wow' when you're not pushing too hard for it."

The technical developments of the last decades have altered the way we work, consume, and communicate. Trigger Happy Productions confront the new requirements with communication measures that are unorthodox and witty enough to overcome the aggravating circumstances of our time. Understanding that "People have become more critical about what is communicated and how," they bank on social skills and turn them into a sustainable marketing advantage: "Clients expect to be taken seriously and want to participate in the communication process. Brand communication has to meet these needs. People don't want to be told what to do or what to buy—therefore the aim of communication should be to communicate at eye-level,

"The most important thing in the collaboration between brand and artist is to find the right partner, someone you share the same general ideas with. This is crucial for both sides. Artists never want to be treated as service providers and brands need be able to trust that the artist's approach fits their idea of themselves."

events and installations for the green energy supplier Entega, Trigger Happy Productions present a range of compelling examples. Conceived of as a creative collaboration and developed to the scope of integrated multimedia campaigns with accompanying print publications, websites, and events-based platforms, their projects approach

and listen to people rather than just dropping a bomb of information; to create a dialogue instead of merely pitching a product."

The real challange of brand communication lies in developing and fostering relationships. This certainly applies to artist-brand collaboration, where the most important thing is to find the right partners and learn to trust them, but also to the relationship between brand and client. Brands are part of our society, and therefore they have to accept social responsibility, but taking on social responsibility shouldn't be directly linked to the brand's economic benefit. Rather than donating money for every yogurt, beer, or water bottle sold, brands should concentrate on being believable in their actions and communication. "To be taken seriously as a brand has a lot to do with taking the people you want to address seriously. You stay relevant as a brand if you take a close look at what's relevant to your clients—and you find out what's relevant to your clients if you listen to what they have to say."

1
Trigger Happy Productions
× Ralf Schmerberg
× DDB for Entega
Holy Wood, 2011

In the framework of a campaign called Denkanstöße, a series of thought-provoking ventures developed by Berlin–based artist Ralf Schmerberg, DDB, and Trigger Happy Productions, German green energy supplier Entega co-partnered with the Berlinale to promote climate protection. The Holy Wood project was launched on the occasion of the 61st Berlin International Film Festival, aiming to reduce the festival's CO_2

balance and to draw attention to the importance of our forests. The initiative included three sub-projects: a large-scale installation adapting the typographical characteristics of the classic Hollywood sign lettering to suit the Berlinale context, the foundation of the ongoing non-profit initiative "10,000 Trees for Berlin," which aims to incite people to plant or adopt trees, and a beautifully-designed book about the forest. The unifying message of all these efforts was that climate protection concerns us all.
Photography: Ralf Schmerberg[1],
Steffen Roth[2]

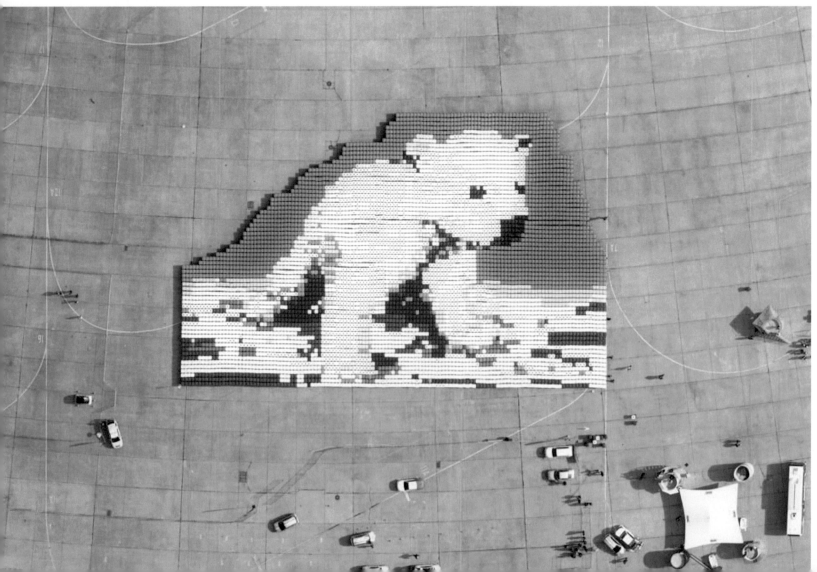

Trigger Happy Productions for BSR
Eisbär, 2010

Berlin's public cleaning service BSR teamed up with the creatives at Trigger Happy Productions and 150 volunteers to build the world's largest mosaic picture on the landing field of the former Tempelhof airport. The huge polar bear the team made was formed from 6500 waste containers. The bear was part of BSR's Trennstadt ("Separation City") campaign, initiated in collaboration with Berlin Recycling, in cooperation with ALBA, an internationally-oriented company working in the waste management and recycling sector, and the Stiftung Naturschutz Berlin. This grand campaign intended to encourage Berlin's citizens to separate their household refuse.

Photography: GeoFly[1], Stephan Vens[2]

2

Trigger Happy Productions

PP. 140–143
Trigger Happy Productions
× Heimat Berlin for Hornbach
**Torstraße 166 - Das Haus der
Vorstellung, 2008**

The key premise of German building
supply store Hornbach became the ral-
lying call of its autumn 2008 campaign:
"You can imagine it. Therefore you can
build it." The campaign started across
classic media channels, with a TV commercial directed by artist Ralf Schmerberg, and then expanded through a variety of media outlets—including a
walkable large-scale installation. For
Das Haus der Vorstellung ("The House
of Imagination"), an abandoned apart-
ment block in the center of Berlin was
transformed into a buzzing platform of
artistic creation. Equipped with Horn-

1

bach materials, twelve artists and creative collectives were invited to realize their individual concepts on the disused premises.

Japanese artist Chiharu Shiota combined the furniture and objects in her flat into an intricate network of threads, and developed an oversized thread installation for the building's façade. The German duo Franz Höfner und Harry Sachs redefined the grammar of conventional home improvement materials, telling satirical DIY and refurbishing stories. The Berlin-based creative architecture collective Plastique Fantastique, famous for their work with pneumatic spaces, joined forces with the audio specialists at Sound and Experience Design to create an impressive video-sound installation featuring giant rubber balloons.

Realized by Trigger Happy Productions on the basis of an idea by creative agency Heimat Berlin, with this initiative the Haus der Vorstellung pushed the boundaries of what advertising can be.

Photography: Max Merz

"We carefully select all our projects and then put our heart and soul into them. We always try to bring together people who will complement and inspire each other. We don't believe in just telling you what you want to hear."

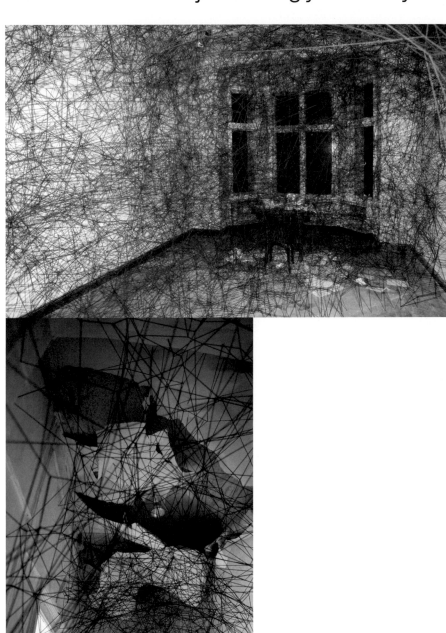

1 2
Chiharu Shiotas, Haus der Vorstellung, 2008. © VG Bild-Kunst, Bonn 2012

3
Souzihaas, Haus der Vorstellung, 2008

Trigger Happy Productions

Portrait

"For a brand to become and stay relevant these days,
it is not only important what, but also how it communicates."

Portrait

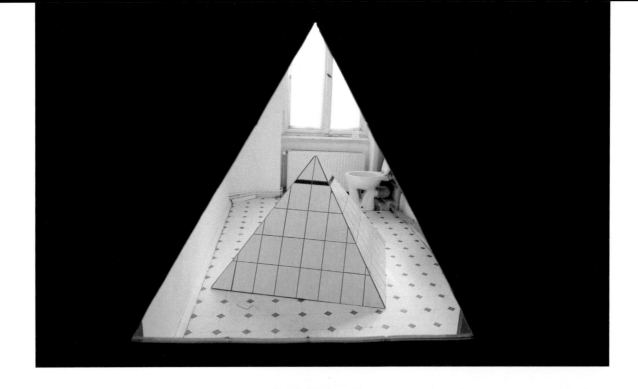

2
Franz Höfner & Harry Sachs, Haus der Vorstellung, 2008

2

Trigger Happy Productions

Trigger Happy Productions
× Ralf Schmerberg
× DDB for Entega
Schneemann Demo, 2010

Under the creative direction of artist Ralf Schmerberg and Berlin-based advertising agency DDB, Trigger Happy Productions realized a public art and information event for the green energy supplier Entega. The group invited the public to build personalized snowmen on an 8,000-square-meter creative snowfield. As a result, a group of 870 individually-designed snowmen marched the streets of Berlin to raise environmental awareness and protect the world against global warming.

The supporting program, hosted by Berlin's Temporäre Kunsthalle, includ-

1

ed a panel discussion with one of Entega's board members, a music performance by Icelandic folk group Seabear, readings of snow and snowman stories by well-known German actress Anna Thalbach, and comprehensive media presentations dealing with central environmental topics.

The project was part of the Denkanstöße campaign, which encompassed a series of thought-provoking projects by Ralf Schmerberg, DDB, and Trigger Happy for Entega.

Photography: Stephan Vens

2
Trigger Happy Productions
x Ralf Schmerberg
x DDB for Entega
Stromfresser, 2010/2011

"Waste is the largest source of energy." That was the statement made by the third thought-provoking project included in German green energy supplier Entega's Denkanstöße campaign. Entega's Stromfresser ("Electricity Guzzler") was a giant igloo consisting of 322 old refrigerators on a steel frame. First set up on the Gänsemarkt

market in Hamburg's historic city center, the walk-in installation traveled to Darmstadt, a midsize German city located in the southern part of the Rhine Region, blowing a whole lot of energy into the air. With a touch of the absurd, the project provided worthwhile food for thought. The igloo was initiated by Berlin-based artist Ralf Schmerberg and the advertising agency DDB, and realized by Trigger Happy for Entega.

Photography: Stephan Vens

"We see ourselves as part of a process in which everything we touch bears the hallmark of our creativity."

2

Nendo for Akio Hirata
Hirata No Boshi, 2011

Commissioned to produce the graphics and exhibition design for the first major Japanese retrospective of internationally-known milliner Hirata Akio at the spiral Garden in Tokyo, the creatives at Nendo configured a space that deserves to be called a piece of art in its own right.

Contrasting Hirata's carefully hand-made hats with a multitude of mass-produced non-woven white hats, which were suspended from invisible threads to hover and float throughout the actual pieces of the exhibition, the designers created a surreal walk-in installation that invites visitors to physically experience Hirata's creations and the creative freedom they are based on.

Photography: Daici Ano

146

MAD Architects for Vertu
Vertu Pavilion, 2011

The design concept of MAD Architects' traveling pavilion for luxury mobile phone maker Vertu is based on the idea of an object crashing to earth from the sky. Inspired by physical principles of nature such as explosion, collision, and the concept of change, the pavilion adapted the aesthetics of meteors and comets. The structure of its façade alludes to post-collision shreds, becoming an homage to the uniqueness of the moment and calling upon the contrast between the old and the new, the local and the foreign, the temporary and the permanent.

Developed to celebrate the release of the Constellation T touchscreen phone, the pavilion served as a temporary gallery space to present Vertu's latest products alongside special videos and touchscreen demonstration.

Designers: Ma Yansong, Dang Qun, Philippe Brysse, Kyle Chou, Tiffany Dahlen, ARUP (Beijing) · Photography: MAD Architects

Serviceplan for BMW
Exceed Maximum, 2010

Commissioned by BMW to develop an impressive advertising solution that would introduce the M3 Coupe to Hamburg airport travelers, Serviceplan Munich set up a huge wall of light in the middle of the airport's arrival hall.

Based on the car maker's claim that the its new creation exceeds limits, Serviceplan designed the billboard to exceed limits, too—namely those of the appointed media space. The billboard's headline, "Exceed Maximum," consists of half-letters that are completed by the airport's shiny floor reflecting the other half.

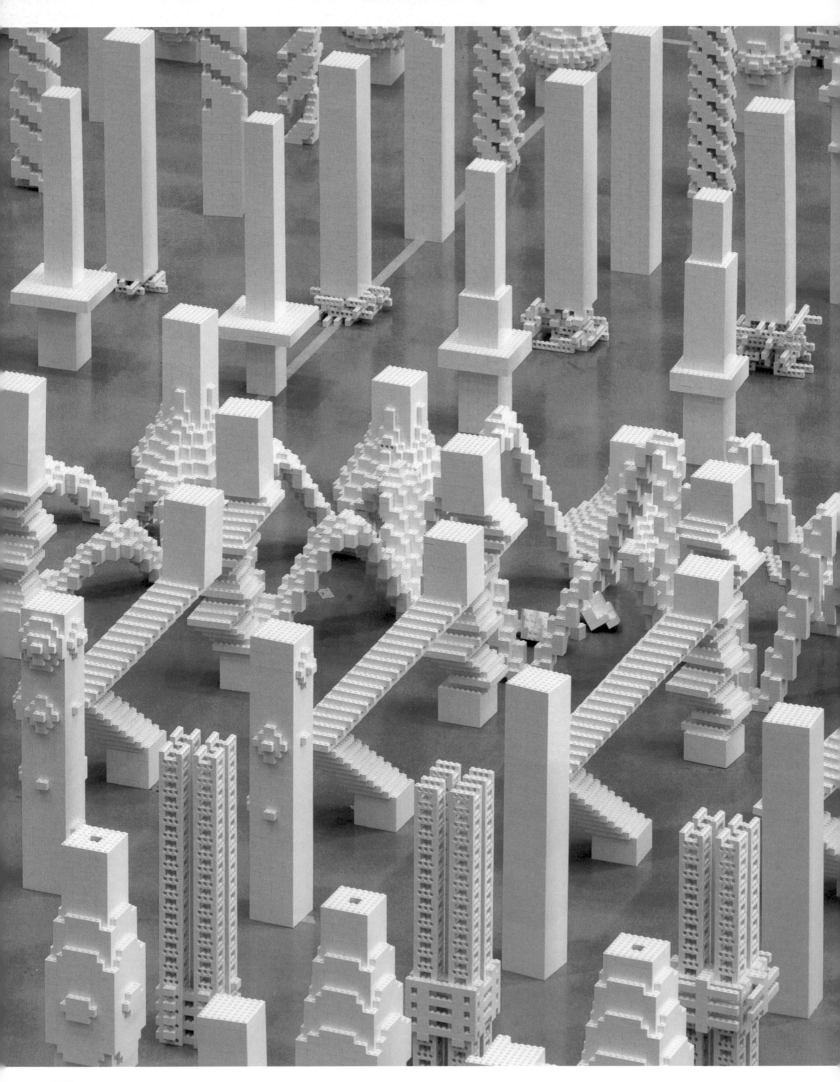

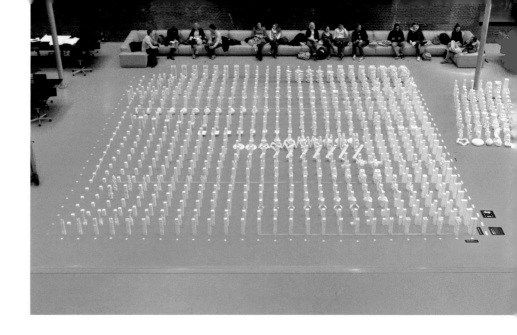

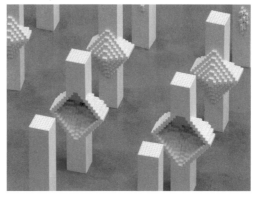

Eurohigh × The Why Factory × KRADS supported by LEGO
Opening the Tower, 2011

Supported by LEGO and the independent creative firm Arup, the participating students used LEGO bricks as a new modeling material to illustrate

Opening the Tower presented the midterm results of Eurohigh, a design studio led by Professor Winy Maas, Alexander Sverdlov and Ania Molenda and developed in collaboration with the young architecture practice KRADS. Working with The Why Factory, the University of Technology at Delft's architecture and urbanism think tank, Eurohigh built up a truly remarkable installation exploring the aspects and potentials of a prototypical European skyscraper and celebrating the power of the pixel to configure a collective entity.

their research results and as a means of fundamental architectural experimentation.

Eurohigh design studio: developed by The Why Factory in collaboration with KRADS, supported by LEGO and Arup   Led by Prof. Winy Maas, Alexander Sverdlov, and Ania Molenda   Participants: Jaap de Jong, Marina Ferrando, Alise Jekabsone, Jayson Johnstone, Valerie Krautzer, Qian LAN, Bill Lee, Albert Mark, Ana Melgarejo, Vincent Paar, Marcus Parviainen, Alex Parvu, Pedro Pitarch, Mihaela Radescu, Marie-lahya Simon, Leo Stuckardt, Calvin Tanikaya and Cyrus Wong   Photography: Frans Parthesius

Sublime Statements

Best Beyond The Line—
Bespoke Items, Premium Editions, and Line Extension

It is a well known irony that items gain popularity when they become rare and hard to get. In a time of instant availability, brands acknowledge the promotional potential of scarcity more than ever before. As a result, they often develop an independent spirit that departs from the mainstream. Brands extend their lines, flooding the market with special issues, limited editions, and custom creations of all kinds—and as if there weren't enough already, these offshoots keep popping up like mushrooms on blogs and the editor's-pick pages of lifestyle magazines. While many examples have come and gone down the path to mass-marketing irrelevance, some are striking and therefore worthy of documentation.

A curiosity cabinet of of contemporary consumer culture, this section gathers innovative creations, conceived of and produced on the basis of high-level craftsmanship and loving attention to detail. This visual investigation aims to reflect the shifting status of the creative product and to redefine its role in the context of a corporate environment that counters mediocrity.

In today's fast-moving consumer industry, competing brands are multitudinous and market conditions harsh. Our readiness to wander is severely limited, our willingness to keep up a relationship with a brand inextricably tied to the feeling of getting something out of the deal. Marketers understand that luxury is about singularity and that winning over the consumer takes much more than rewarding someone with discounts and client gifts. Creative makers know that the notion of "noteworthiness" has undergone a redefinition. The contemporary customer has developed an appetite for more culturally-complex goods. In an attempt to meet this craving, brands, designers, and artists from various fields team up and work out eclectic responses, which often end with quite a high aesthetic value.

Some projects impress us with creative energy and inventive talent, like Rolf Sachs's ^{P. 167} Davoser sleds, or Zarb's ^{PP. 174–175} limited edition champagne bottles designed by THEY and a couple of fellow creatives. Some merge traditional material and craftsmanship with cutting edge design to bring about peculiar creations, 5.5 Designers' ^{PP. 170–171} collection of silverware baby gifts for Richard, for example. Others present themselves as beautiful objects of temptation with extraordinary packaging, compilation, and make-up, like Owen & Stork's

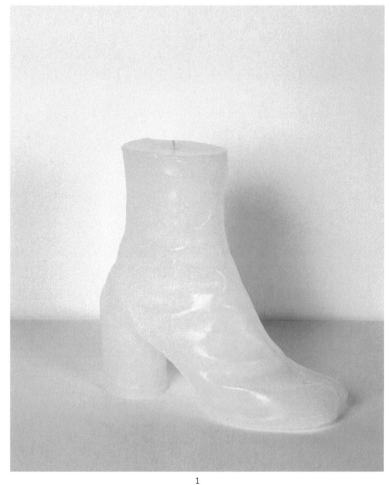

1

2

P. 168 Grooming Kit for the Portland General Store. Again others are highly coveted for the sake of celebrity authorship.

Made available only for a select few, specialty products like these do not only signify exclusivity and affiliation (for those among the lucky few), but also flatten the line between art and consumer goods, between high and popular culture. What is more is that they blur the notion of the actual product with the mythical haze that surrounds it. Unavailable or in limited supply to the general public, a large part of these items predominantly speak to those who are themselves voices of the industry: a strategically picked group of press, bloggers, stylists, buyers, and photographers, happy to promote the message of aspiration and to publicly profess allegiance. The professional background and trade-specific style awareness of the visually-trained target group raises expectations. As a result, marketing departments, designers, artists, and manufacturers work to the limit, max out their skills in order to create something outstanding that will, first and foremost, generate public response.

Predominantly conceived of as tools of self-expression, some of the projects in this section have no immediate commercial application whatsoever. Although almost all are initiated by brands, their main objective is not to sell. They are, rather, designed to promote sales (of certain products, ideas, and services) or the broader brand itself, to which the perceived positive aura of the exceptional item extends. It is through this "halo effect," a prominent psychological phenomenon that examples found in all four sections of this book are based on, that these "halo items" bear fruit, however intangible it is.

From a creative perspective, "halo items" are highly desirable projects to work on. Not part of a standard product range or main line that can make or break a business, these items celebrate a certain independence from default production parameters and requisite sales figures. As a result, more lee-way is granted to the designers and artists working on the project. Expected to innovate and experiment, they often enjoy considerable creative freedom—not only in regards to the project brief, but also in terms of budget.

However controversial, many unorthodox endeavors prove worthwhile. Neatly merchandised and often transcending brief purposes to become cherished cult and collector items, these projects not only represent a long-term investment in the brand, but add a new dimension to the creative world.

Photography: Nienke Klunder

3

Maison Martin Margiela

PP.

156–163

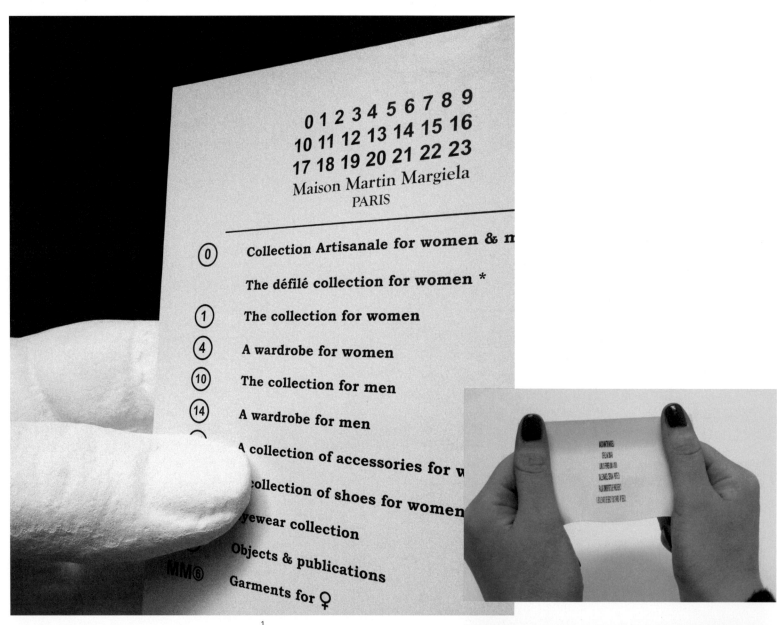

1

1 | PP. 160–161
Maison Martin Margiela
"20" The Exhibition, 2008/2009/2010

2
Maison Martin Margiela
Show Invitation, 2008

To invite selected guests to Margiela's autumn/winter show in 2008, the design house created beautiful invitations. Each invitation was formed from a sheet of rubber with condensed text on it. The information on the invitation only become readable once the rubber was expanded.

Photography: Maison Martin Margiela

2

A graduate of Belgium's Royal Academy of Fine Arts, where he studied along with the legendary avant-garde fashion collective The Antwerp Six, Martin Margiela launched his career as a design assistant at Jean Paul Gaultier in 1984. Causing a real shift in fashion by introducing confounding garments and techniques, he presented the first collection under his own label in 1989, and became one of the most eminent players on the global fashion stage. And yet Margiela has worked with great anonymity, directing public rather a bonus, which must be relevant to the collection and be based solidly in the brand, arising naturally. "Only then it can be successful and effective," Margiela states. "The Maison Margiela creates other product categories or works in other domains, always thinking of the fashion product as the main reference for the entire brand frame."

However effective these "other product categories or works in other domains" are in regards to fashion products, MMM's core business and the related sales numbers are certainly hard to measure. There may not even be an

"We work hard, as many other fashion houses do, to create original works that can provoke thoughts, pleasure, and appreciation."

attention away from himself as a person and instead towards his designs, allowing them to speak for themselves. Instead of claiming ownership, Margiela sets great store by the fact that his collections are the achievement of a collaborative team.

His legacy is an all-white island of understatement surrounded by the turbulent streams of the fashion industry. Handed over to the Diesel Group Maison Martin Margeila has gained mainstream appeal in recent years. New product lines, like sunglasses and fragrances, have been introduced. The anonymous collaborative spirit and distinct brand visual identity remained.

All correspondence from the company is written in the plural, signed "Maison Martin Margiela." At the Maison's Paris atelier, housed in the premises of an old school building in the 11th Arrondissement, everything—from furniture to walls to staff members—is veiled in light white fabric, countering an egocentric fashion world with a sense of washed-out collectivity. Stripped of visual distraction, the Margiela style suggests a pleasant honesty and entails a silence that provides room for self-reflection.

After all, a brand is more than the physical characteristics of its products. For Maison Martin Margiela, the brand is an "ensemble of values," an entire world of references for an audience and its perceptions. Achieving consistency within this world has likely been the most difficult hurdle. Margiela's rigorous identity concept yields cohesive "extras" season after season, for example, a range of non-fashion products, brand events, and print publications. In 2011, La Maison Champs-Elysees opened, a mostly-white hotel that was redesigned by MMM. However, the Maison does not consider line extension a must,

immediate commercial application for all of them. The accent is really on the notion of something existing beyond all that, something that is of high perceived value although not always clearly assigned to a certain functions or product categories: brand oevre that exists in the mythical halo of particularity and is therefore worth talking about.

While the fashion world continuously demands creative innovation and specialties, the term "special edition" has long come and gone down the path to mass-marketing irrelevance. But MMM never used it anyway. "The Maison tries to make all its products a specialty, a special experience for its customer, so the trend for special edition products is not really part of Margiela's DNA." Undeterred by harsh market conditions, jaded consumers, and the ever-present claim to "Reframe! Create! Differentiate!" MMM focuses on fostering and refining Margiela's passed-down identity, and has managed to stay different. The team thinks it must be due to their will to create an honest, genuine vision, and to work according to a sort of consistency in all their formal expressions. "We work hard, as many other fashion houses do, to create original works that provoke thought, pleasure and appreciation—something that we hope is meaningful for our public." MMM has never worked hard to gain cult status, though, understanding that such agendas seldom work. "It is easier to achieve that status when you do things you like and you are good at, with extreme passion and freedom."

Certainly a cult factor is MMM's sense of longevity, which extends far beyond seasonal trends. After looking back through the entire body of work to put together the extensive retrospective "20" and its accompanying book, MMM reflects on the most challenging, but also most rewarding project it's ever done: "We had a hard time selecting, but we were happy with the result, lots of memories...but nothing in comparison with tomorrow's work, which always presents itself as more challenging and hopefully very rewarding."

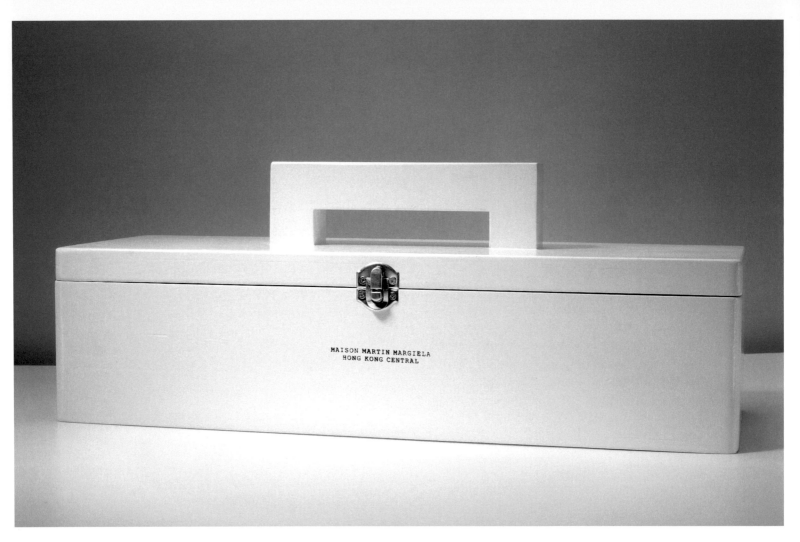

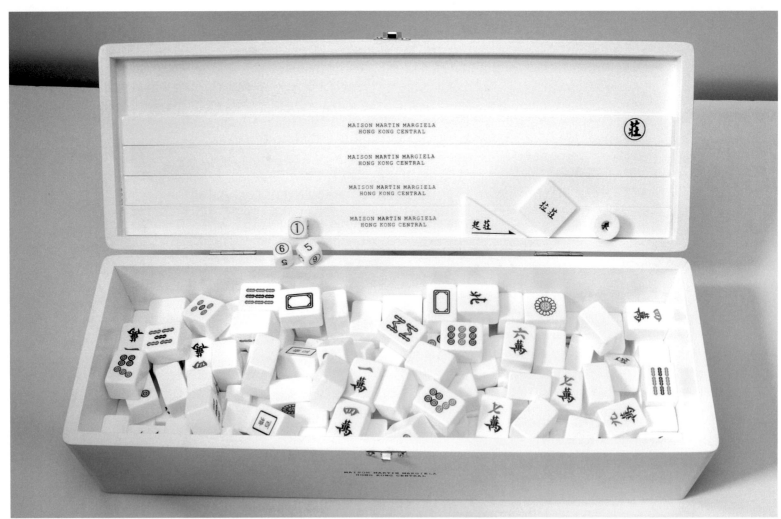

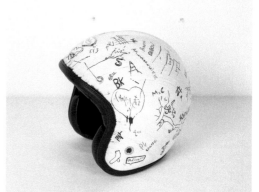

2

1
Maison Martin Margiela
Mahjong Set, 2009

Maison Martin Margiela's Hong Kong anniversary celebration took place at the label's On Lan Street store in central Hong Kong. The event was commemorated with a regionally-relevant item: a special and limited edition set of mahjong tiles to be given away to selected customers. Custom-crafted by Maison Martin Margiela, the board game and its box are all white, washed in the brand's signature (non-)color. The mahjong lining ruler comes with a black custom "Maison Martin Margiela Hong Kong Central" inscription.

2
Maison Martin Margiela
× Les Ateliers Ruby
Helmet, 2009

For the third edition of Les Ateliers Ruby's "Signature" program, the deluxe helmet maker's founder Jérôme Coste wanted to venture into the off-beat and interpretive territory of Maison Martin Margiela.

Highly enthusiastic about the prospect of creating a Ruby helmet, the iconic fashion house took the program title literally and came up with a team piece incorporating the signatures of Martin Margiela and his colleagues at the Paris studio.

In the course of customization, the carbon shell was varnished and then covered with broad lines of paint, creating a whitewashed effect that stays true to the Maison's hallmark of pure white color schemes. Margiela's design team's names are engraved into the painted layer, contrasting slightly yet visibly against the white. The traditional Les Ateliers Ruby cardinal red interior was replaced by black leather, creating a strong visual punch.

Photography: Julien Oppenheim / MMM

"You can now ride in peace. The whole of Maison Martin Margiela is with you."

"A brand is an ensemble of values... an entire world of references for an audience and its perception."

Maison Martin Margiela
"20" The Exhibition, 2008/2009/2010

First shown at MoMu in Antwerp, then at Haus der Kunst in Munich, and finally at Somerset House in London, Maison Martin Margiela's multi-layered exhibition "20" captures the brand's unique aesthetic vision and the history of its unfolding over the past 20 years. Incorporating installations, photography, video, and film, the show provided an opportunity to experience the brand and its philosophy through a visual examination of themes that have underpinned the essence of the fashion house since its creation. The visual history moves from Margiela's deconstructivist, subversive design aesthetic and avant-garde couture to its understated branding, unusual boutique interiors, trompe-l'oeil effects, and couture atelier white coats. On display were various iconic pieces from previous collections, plus a range of special garments produced exclusively for the exhibition.

Photography: Sylvain Deleu, Ronald Stoops, Koerg Koopman / MMM

Maison
MARTIN
MARGIELA
20
THE EXHIBITION
SOMERSET HOUSE
3 JUNE – 5 SEPT. 2010

www.somersethouse.org.uk/margiela

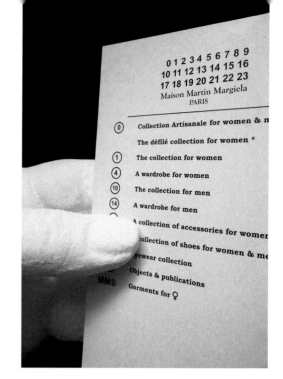

MM
MODEMUSEUM

FASHION MUSEUM ANTWERP
PRESENTS

MAISON MARTIN MARGIELA *proper noun, plural,* derived from the name of a Belgian stylist. **Fashion company** created in **Paris** in 1988. Registered office situated at number 163 rue Saint Maur, 75011, Paris. Known for its taste for **transgression**, its fashion shows in unexpected places, its "street casting" mixing all ages. Categorised successively as underground, deconstructive, destroy, grunge, minimalist, provocative, established. ♦ **1°** Garments for women, offering several collections, from ready-to-wear fashion to unique pieces (*Artisanal* collection). The main collection uses a plain *white label** with no writing, sewn into the garments by hand with four *white stitches**. The other collections, of which there are 12, are identified by a circled number on the label. ♦ **2°** Male clients have also been taken care of since 1998, with four distinct collections. ♦ **3°** Communicates exclusively in the first person plural "we", in order to focus attention on *teamwork** (16 nationalities) and to respect the creator's wish for *anonymity**: *"The only thing we wish to push to the fore-front is our fashion"*. ♦ **4°** Known for its taste for *recovery** and *recycling** of materials. ♦ **5°** May go as far as to re-release an existing garment (*Replicas**). ♦ **6°** Since its creation, has favoured the use of *whites**: walls, floors, stands, accessories, hanging wardrobes, in its boutiques, showrooms and offices. ♦ **7°** Its employees wear *white coats** (from "haute couture" workshops) as a "uniform" when serving the public. ♦ **8°** *Ext.* Sunglasses, jewellery, perfumes. ♦ **9°** A study subject in fashion schools. ♦ **10°** Name used internationally in books, articles and exhibitions.

⑳ THE EXHIBITION *proper noun, singular.* ♦ **1°** Exhibition to celebrate the 20 years of Maison Martin Margiela, from **September 12, 2008** to **February 8, 2009**. ♦ **2°** Taking place at **MoMu, Nationalestraat 28**, in **Antwerp**.

WWW.MOMU.BE

161

Maison Martin Margiela

"The consistency of several activities, products, and services carried out by a brand is likely the hardest challenge to achieve."

Maison Martin Margiela × Colette

**Maison Martin Margiela @ Colette,
2009 – 2010**

Colette invited Maison Martin Margiela to whiten Colette's corner space and use it as a venue to celebrate the launch of its Line 13.

Margiela brought giant snowballs, matryoshka dolls, fabric calendars, bottle lamps, goose and ostrich feather fountain pens, jewelry from Line 12, and—exclusively for Colette—the re-issue of the vintage wool and chiffon scarf from the 1999 Artisanal collection, two unique Swarovski crystallized items, the Maison Martin Margiela book published by Rizzoli and Flammarion, and the label's famous white cotton bag.

As part of the project, MMM turned Colette's carrier bags into rare collector's items that were given away to pre-Christmas shoppers.

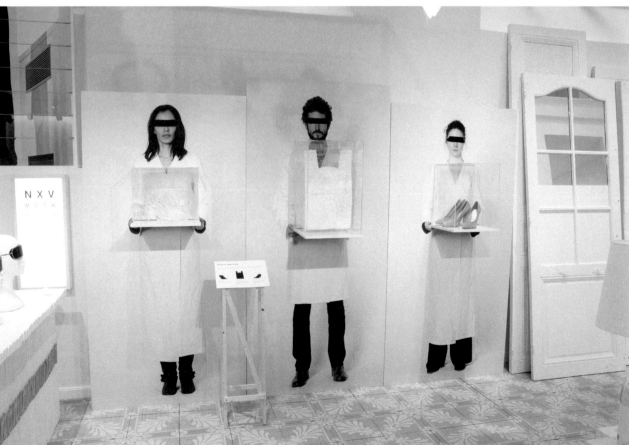

Ace Hotel
× The Impossible Project
Impossible Ace Edition, 2011

Ace Hotels create locations to touch the senses of travelers, hedonists, artists, and adventurers. The Impossible Project manufactures new instant film for vintage Polaroid cameras to revive the tangible magic of analog instant photography. Sharing the common desire to reinvent the power of the moment and create unique experiences, Ace Hotels and The Impossible Project partnered to create an instant film edition. Designed in the characteristic Ace style by the designers of Atelier Ace, the Impossible PX 600 Silver Shade film comes in a high-quality box with a removable lid. The limited-edition custom packs of PX 600 Silver Shade instant black & white film were offered in the mini−bars of Ace Hotel New York guest rooms and other Ace Hotel locations, and at The Impossible Project Spaces in Vienna, Tokyo, and New York, as well as online.

The project was accompanied by a introductory booklet, a refurbished original Polaroid camera, and the exhibition 24 Hours at Ace, featuring Impossible Photos by Adam Goldberg, Andie Acosta, Anne Bowerman, Araks Yeramyan, Chloe Aftel, Dave Ortiz, Devon Turnbull, Elijah Wood, Jeremy Kost, Michael Nevin, Nicole Held, Pat Sansone, and Steve Olson.

Photography: Impossible

164

For Thomas Erber's Cabinet of Curiosities, a traveling show bringing together a variety of artists and brands
to create lovingly-produced specialty products, Alexander Olch, makers of
fine silk, cashmere, and woolen neck-
ties, presented a maple wood engraved
box containing a matching set of exclusive contents. Inside could be found: a
necktie, a bowtie, a pocket round, sus-
penders, and a notebook, all handmade
in New York and shown exclusively in
the framework of Thomas Erber's Cabinet of Curiosities at Colette in Paris.

Photography: Alexander Olch

Shwood
x Pendleton Woolen Mills
Canby Wooden Sunglasses, 2011

Shwood, a maker of wood-framed sunglasses, joined forces with fellow Oregon-based company Pendleton Woolen Mills to create a limited run of the popular "Canby" frame style. Crafted from Oregon-grown cherry wood, the frame features laser-engraved temples adorned with Pendleton's iconic "Chief Joseph" pattern. Taking the collaboration a step further, Pendleton manufactured a matching carrying pouch woven from a limited batch of wool exclusive to the project. With both parties dedicated to domestic manufacturing, the project pays tribute to their home state of Oregon and their heritage manufacturing techniques.

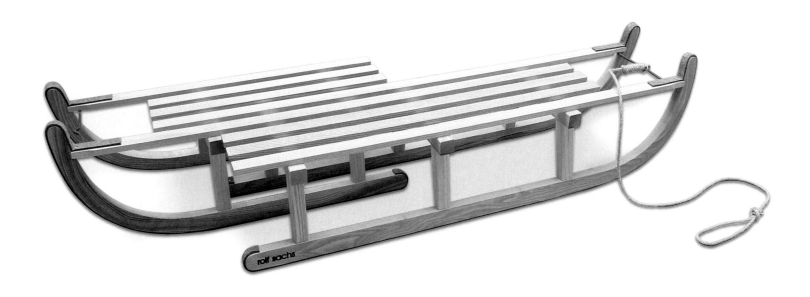

Rolf Sachs
Insepar-able, 2010

Swiss artist Rolf Sachs took two classic Davoser ash hardwood sleds and fused them together like an inseparable couple. The result is a surreal, sculptural piece that can either be used as a coffee table or as a seating accommodation, bringing back memories of playful bygone days in the snow.

Two prior models of sledges were produced in 2004.

Photography: Bryon Slater

1
Owen & Stork for
Portland General Store
Grooming Kit, 2011

For their first brand collaboration, the designers of creative agency Owen & Stork teamed up with men's grooming supply company Portland General Store. The result is a very limited edition of 12 handmade kits, bringing together some of Portland General Store's most popular grooming products with custom packaging and tools. Designed not only to function but to continue looking better with age, the product interprets the gentleman's vanity with a whole bunch of good humor.

Hardly any of the kits were intended to be sold; the majority were given away as gifts to both stockists and relevant publications.

2
Good Wood
× All Things Fresh for Drake
Drake's Birthday Gift Box, 2011

Good Wood and All Things Fresh teamed up to design a memorable gift set celebrating the 25th birthday of Canadian musician and actor Drake. The wooden box is assembled and painted by hand, its inside upholstered in velvet and subdivided into layers and compartments to fit the individual products: shot glasses, necklaces, bracelets, iPhone 4 cases, and a couple of owls, which are the logo for Drake's brand, October's Very Own. Showcasing an array of capabilities, Good Wood made use of CO_2 laser engravers and various woodworking tools. The signage is made of stained inlays constructed to form Drake's owl logo.

Photography: David Ross · Additional credits: Thomas Dudley, Cassandra Baker

1

5.5 Designers for Richard
Bienvenue!, 2011

To celebrate its centenary, the traditional French goldsmiths at Richard launched the Welcome! series and invited a selection of new talents from the contemporary creative scene to reinterpret a collection of sterling silver flatware. Amongst them was the collective 5.5 Designers, who shook up Richard's traditional style to formulate a collection of whimsical silverware that revisits classic baby gifts in a fun, yet technically sophisticated way. The result was a curious and humorous antithesis to mass-manufactured products and a passionate tribute to the arts and crafts.

Courtesy of 5.5 Designers

The Motley
× The Spare Room
Dopp Kit, 2011

Superior men's grooming brand The Motley worked with the head mixologist at The Spare Room, a cocktail bar and gaming room in Hollywood's Roosevelt Hotel, to recreate the key elements of a classic gin and tonic with pure essential oils, creating the ultimate bath experience for cocktail lovers—gin and tonic bath salts. The result is part of a limited edition Dopp Kit, produced with loving attention to detail. The handcrafted leather and canvas bags for the collaboration were created by Draught Dry Goods, a small Portland-based company dedicated to the crafts of high-quality sewing and leather working.

Baxter of California × Porter Japan
Grooming Implements, 2011

Co-designed in-house by premium men's grooming line Baxter of California and luxury bag maker Porter Japan as a collaborative branded product, the limited edition Grooming Kit consists of a Denier Nylon Twill outer shell, a durable Denier Cordura Nylon Ox lining, and shock-proof padding to protect its contents. Inside are a set of high-quality tools, such as German Solingen tweezers, a stainless steel nail clipper, and a long-lasting tempered glass nail file.

Tying in with Porter's commitment to create fantastic, elaborate luggage, a matte black YKK symmetric zipper enables the user to close the bag smoothly—in any direction, whether upward, downward, left or right.

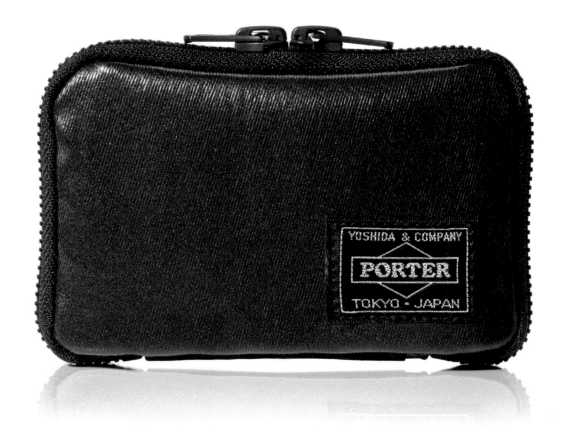

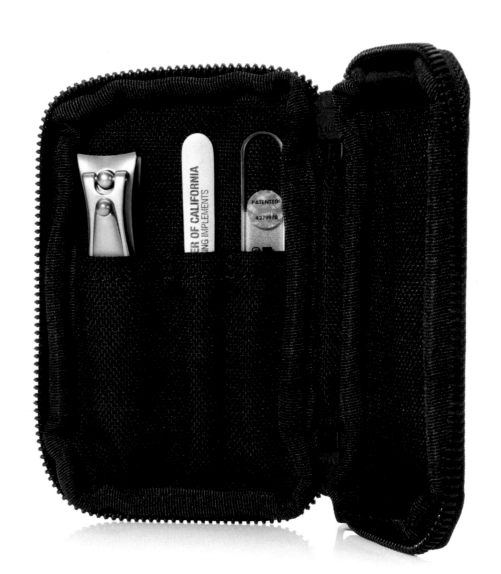

1
THEY and Zarb

3
THEY × EDHV

5
THEY × Tjep.

2
THEY × Hans Aarsman

4
THEY × La Bolleur

6
THEY × Cornelie Tollens
Skin collection "Lips"

1

3

5

2

4

6

7
THEY × Zarb

8
THEY × Zena Holloway
Deep Black Series "Angels"

9
THEY × Zarb

10
THEY × Zena Holloway
Deep Black Series "Surface"

Costume designer: Vin Burnham

11
THEY × Miktor & Molf

**THEY x Various Artist for
Zarb Champagne**
Zarb Art Bottles, 2000 – 2011

Given that its brand name is a French colloquialism for "bizarre," the world of Zarb Champagne is a weird one in which the bottles are king.

Following a creative concept by the Amsterdam-based communications agency THEY, ten artists, including Zarb's creatives, designed a range of distinct magnum bottles for the brand. Among the participants were Hans Aarsman, EDHV, La Bolleur, Miktor & Molf, Tjep, and THEY themselves, whose creation, entitled Straight Black, features Zarb drawing the sword to salute Napoleon's attitude towards champagne: "In victory, you deserve champagne; in defeat, you need it."

All special edition art bottles were exhibited in Zarb's own pop-up store and gallery.

7

9

8

10

11

Sagmeister Inc. for J. & L. Lobmeyr
Drinking Set No.248 - Seven Deadly Sins and Seven Heavenly Virtues, 2011

In this collaboration between Sagmeister Inc. for J. & L. Lobmeyr, it would be possible to mention a silent partner: the Austrian architect Adolf Loos. The project was triggered by the 80th anniversary of Loos's legendary No. 248 bar set. On this occasion, designers Stefan Sagmeister and Jessica Walsh picked up on an idea Loos had approached Lobmeyr with in May 1931: in a letter that recovered from the company archive, Loos asked to replace the bar set's original geometric patterns with "butterflies, small animals and the nude human form" on the bottom of the glasses. Sagmeister and Walsh expanded upon Loos's concept with the use of the Seven Deadly Sins and Heavenly Virtues, which brought with it a rich theme for the illustrations, and the possibility to start a discussion about good and evil at the dinner table. The individual images reveal themselves at the bottom of each glass as it is emptied.

Juan-les Pins, den 22.V.1931.
Palais Wilson.

An die Fa.

J.& L. L o b m e y r   W i e n I.

Sehr geehrter Herr Rath !

Ich erhielt vorgestern Ihren Brief vom 18.d.M. und erst heute die beiden Gläser. Mit Muster "B" bin ich einverstanden, folgendes wünsche ich geändert. Genau senkrechte Seite, welche mit der Bodenfläche einen r e c h t e n Winkel und daher eine starke Kante bildet. Die Bodenfläche möglichst eben und n i c h t konkav. Im Übrigen bin ich mit diesem Modell sehr zufrieden ! Was nun die Grösse der einzelnen Gläser betrifft, so glaube ich,dass das eingesandte Musterglas als Weinglas gerade richtig ist, auf keinen Fall aber grösser werden soll. Der Stand eines Achtels soll aussen mit einem wagrechten Strich angezeichnet werden.(Achtung.). Die Grösse der Übrigen Gläser Überlasse ich Ihrer Erfahrung.

Ich würde es sehr begrüssen, wenn das ganze Service noch in Köln ausgestellt werden könnte, wo mitte Juli eine Ausstellung mit einem von mir eingerichtetem Speisezimmer eröffnet wird. Ich bitte Sie daher der Ausstellungsfirma (Gebrüder Schürmann,Köln/Rhein,Zeppelinhaus) ein Preisoffert für Wiederverkäufer für das komplette Service zu schikken, sobald dies Ihnen möglich sein wird. Ich wünsche euch,das Sie das Service zum Musterschutz anmelden und erwarte Ihre

- 2 -

entsprechenden Vorschläge.

Nun kann ich Ihnen auch meine neuen Ideen mitteilen. An Stelle der viereckigen Facetten sechs- oder achteckige. --- Unter dem Boden ein gefärbtes Ueberfangglas : weiss (Champagner), feueropal (Rotwein), lichtgrün (Weisswein), in dieses Ueberfangglas wird das Muster eingeschliffen, Boden g l a t t , mit eingeschliffenen kleinen Motiven : Schmetterling, Fliege,menschliche nackte Figur, kleine Tiere usw.----

Ich hoffe bald Neues von Ihnen zu hören und verbleibe Ihr ergebener

Adolf Loos m.p.

Die beiden Gläser sende ich per Post zurück.

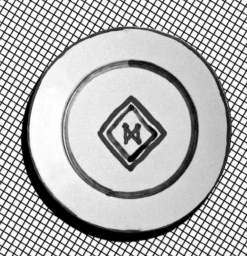

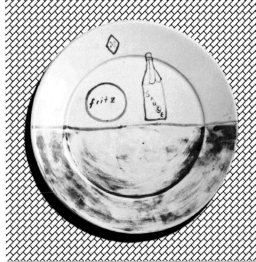

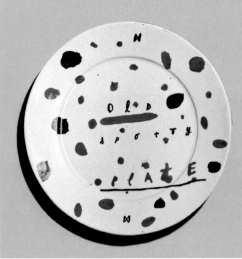

1

2

**Eduardo Sarabia for
Other Criteria**
18 With a Bullet, 2009

The series of hand-painted ceramic vases Eduardo Sarabia produced for
and with Other Criteria refers to the artist's Mexican heritage and intentionally
parodies the cultural clichés surrounding drug smuggling, illegal trade, and
machismo. On the vases one can find
illegal contraband motifs, busty naked
ladies, cannabis leaves, and hand guns,
in addition to more traditional elements
of decoration. The 2009 edition consists
of 18 unique multiples, each in its own
painted wooden box.

Photography: Other Criteria Ltd   © the artist

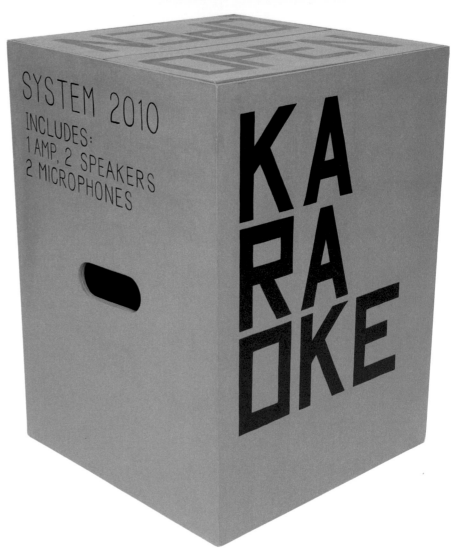

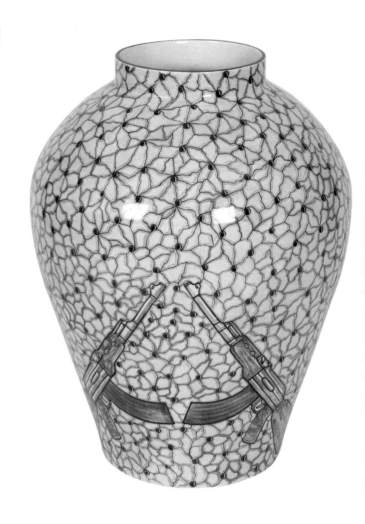

1

1
Jorge Julián Aristizábal for Artware Editions
Plates, 2008

There are dozens of different hand-drawn images decorating these oven-fired ceramic plates by Colombian artist Jorge Julián Aristizábal. The subjects, often existential or sexual in nature, derive directly from large-format pencil drawings that are part of the artist's larger oeuvre. All plates are signed and dated by the artist and available from Artware Editions in three sizes.

Courtesy of Artware Editons, NYC

2
Cindy Sherman for Artware Editions
Madame de Pompadour (née Poisson), 1990

Renowned artist and photographer Cindy Sherman created this 30-piece Limoges porcelain dinner service in a limited edition, based on an original design commissioned by Madame de Pompadour (née Poisson) in 1756 at the Manufacture Royale de Sèvres. The self-portrait image of the artist as Madame de Pompadour was transferred onto porcelain through a complex process requiring up to 16 photo-silkscreens. Each dinner plate was silkscreened and painted at Ancienne Manufacture Royale. The service includes six each of presentation plates, dinner plates, salad plates, rimmed soup bowls, and dessert plates, and is available in four traditional 18th century colors: apple green, rose, royal blue, and yellow. Each color set was created in an edition of 75.

Published by Artes Magnus. Courtesy of Artware Editions, NYC and Artes Magnus

3
John Gerrard for Artware Editions
Bone Cutlery, 2009

For Artware Editions, Irish artist John Gerrard created Bone Cutlery, a set of silver-plated flatware and a pair of silver-plated salad tossers. As with much of Gerrard's work, Bone Cutlery furthers the artist's inquiry into the underlying structures that sustain us, in this case, the frequently opaque systems intrinsic to food production and consumption by which food ar-

2

3

182

rives at our tables. The handles for the Bone Cutlery flatware and the entire forms of the salad tossers are molded directly from different bones of a single goat. Gerrard collaborated closely with traditional silversmiths in the south of France to pair bone handles with classic heads so that each of the pieces is properly weighted and feels comfortable in-hand. The pieces are then plated with 33-micron silver and have a mirror-like finish, making the forms at once primal and alluring.

Courtesy of Jakob Polacsek and Artware Editions, NYC

4 5 6
Amanda Lepore for Artware Editions
Amanda, 2008

Amanda is a boutique fragrance by American model, nightclub hostess, fashion icon, performance artist, and transgender icon Amanda Lepore. Designed by award-winning perfumer Christophe Laudamiel of Les Christophs, the scent is expertly and exquisitely crafted. The assertive blonde-wood structure imparts a warm amber tone with beautiful floral extracts like tuberose, orris butter, violet, and orange flowers. The achieved

smooth, velvety whiteness reminiscent of Amanda's soft, white skin combines with elegant citrus inspired by an Italian Renaissance elixir to give the fragrance a golden shimmer reinforced with a sliver of Cristal champagne. For quirkiness, there is a dash of cucumber and strawberry and a stroke of red lipstick. Released in a limited edition of 5,000 Swarovski-jeweled bottles, Amanda comes in a case lined with black satin that includes a blush-colored satin atomizer and a signed booklet featuring new photographs of Ms. Lepore by acclaimed photographer Nico Iliev.

Courtesy of Andrew Giammarco Studio[5], Nico Iliev[6], and Artware Editions, NYC

5

4

6

1

1
Sebastian Menschhorn
for J. & L. Lobmeyr
Serie Gletscher, 2005

The Vienna-based designer Sebastian Menschhorn collaborated with Lobmeyr to produce a sculptural glass vase with a truly remarkable surface. Manifesting Menschhorn's archaic, open-minded approach to the material, the 10-kilo object resembles a chunk of ice cut from a glacier. Although it is the result of an elaborate grinding process, the raw, chiseled edges suggest naturalness and purity.

On the occasion of its 181st anniversary, Lobmeyr produced 181 handmade Sebastian Menschhorn vases.

2
Philippe Malouin
for J. & L. Lobmeyr
Installation for Passionswege at Vienna Design Week, 2011

The concept of time is key to Lobmeyr's corporate philosophy. Not only do Lobmeyr's glass objects possess timeless design elements independent of changing fashions, but the caliber of the crystal itself ensures that they will stand the test of time. Furthermore, great investments of time are made in producing and decorating the crystal—up to 100 hours for a single object. Philippe Malouin picked up on the theme of time, and developed an installation to represent Lobmeyr within the context of Passionswege, a Vienna Design Week forum that invites young, emerging designers to work with selected Vienna-based firms and manufacturers.

Inspired by the flow of sand through an hourglass, the machine dispenses sand, not to mark minutes and hours, but to form abstract transient patterns. Illustrating the link between time and material, the sand is also particularly significant for Lobmeyr's product range, since it is the raw material from which crystal is created.

2

Pierre Gonalons
for Kiehl's
Silver Recovery, 2009

Pierre Gonalons's Silver Recovery line for Kiehl's is based on the concept of upcycling. Celebrating sustainability, the designer and artistic director of Ascète Studio gave a second life to Kiehl's empty product containers, covering them with pure silver by means of traditional mirror silvering techniques.

SILVER RECOVERY

ASCÈTE FOR *Kiehl's*

DESIGN PIERRE GONALONS

Kiehl's has long been offering its customers the possibility to return used packaging for recycling. Inviting Pierre Gonalons to transform and magnify these containers, Kiehl's allows for their clients' refuse to become the material for a futuristic silversmith's work.

Using only two forms of Kiehl's identity packaging, Gonalons created the iconic vases, Crown Pillar and Pyramid, adopting the names of two ancient symbols of longevity.

1

2

1
LAQ × Jean-Charles de Castelbajac
Mingskatable, 2011

Specializing in the creation of unique, high-quality crafted objects, Raphael Lancrey Javal and Pascal Maugein of LAQ linked up with Jean-Charles de Castelbajac to create a fairly unconventional limited edition table. Born from the clash between the ancient art of Chinese lacquering and contemporary urban culture, the Mingskatable is a free and radical piece of sculptural furniture bearing reference to the Ming Era. Its shiny glaze consists of seven layers of black and sandal lacquer on maple wood. The edition is limited to only eight pieces.

© VG Bild-Kunst, Bonn 2012

2
Alessi x ForeverLamp
AlessiLux, 2011,

Another bright idea by Alessi: AlessiLux is about experimentation, creative ventures, and developing a new approach to lighting. Constantly on the lookout for new design challenges, Alessi joined forces with Foreverlamp to enter a new product sector, and the uncharted territory of the design light bulb. Detached from the lamp and its fixtures, the focus of the piece is on the bulb itself and its variety of shapes and colors. The object, which plays at the border between lamp and bulb, results in expressive creations—way too interesting to be tucked away under a lampshade. The collection consists of seven LED lamp designs, each available in either 55 or 75 watts.

Putting its own designers (primarily Giovanni Alessi Anghini, Gabriele Chiave, and Frederic Gooris) in charge of the creative lead of the project, Alessi entrusted Foreverlamp with the production and distribution of the AlessiLux Collection, harnessing the lighting company's expertise and extensive know-how of the field.

The result of the collaboration is aesthetically and technically first-rate, and exemplary in regards to sustainability standards.

AlessiLux is only the beginning of a series of upcoming Alessi lighting collections.

Design: Giovanni Alessi Anghini, Gabriele Chiave

Pierre Gonalons for
Pernod Absinthe
Cube Bar, 2011

Inspired by glamorous home bars of the Art Deco era and the fluid female forms of Art Nouveau, Pierre Gonalons realized a series of service objects for Pernod Absinthe, the iconic drink much appreciated by the artists and dandies of the elegant Belle Epoque for its unique intoxicating effects. Combining heavy metal and blown glass, the designer and artistic director of Ascète Studio developed a collection that includes a fountain, an absinthe spoon, and a spray that can be distributed all over the world to the finest hotels, bars, and restaurants. Gonalons's Cube Bar compiles a new collection of service objects, aiming to revive the symbol of the French art de vivre with its modernized, straight-lined design.

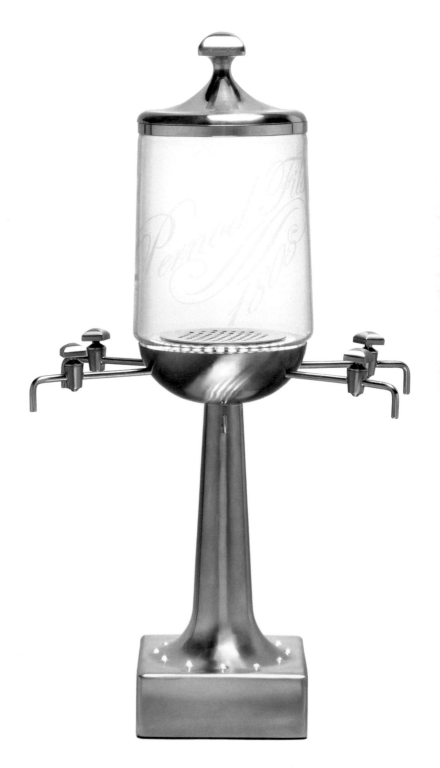

Sociedad Anónima for Perrier
Societé Perrier, 2011

Looking to improve its market position in Mexico, Perrier entrusted Sociedad Anónima to get rid of the stigma of an "inaccessible" product and introduce Perrier as a fun brand for everyone. As a response, the Mexico City-based designers staged a Perrier brand event and invited the new target group to become part of it.

The so-called Societé Perrier featured branded lounge chairs designed by Oscar Hagerman, lounge lamps by Sociedad Anónima and Ricardo Casas, a custom poster collage and neon installation, Perrier coolers, and a Perrier Volkswagen Beetle with pattern design made up of Mexican fighting "gallos"—all created in order to link the European brand to Mexican culture.

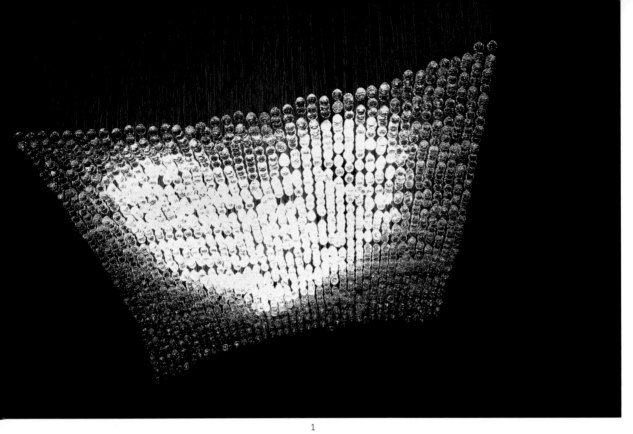

1

2
Moritz Waldemeyer
× Yves Béhar for Swarovski
and Bombay Sapphire
Voyage, 2005

Created for Swarovski and Bombay Sapphire and later installed at New York's John F. Kennedy International Airport, the Voyage chandelier is composed of 52,000 crystals and 2,000 LEDs attached to a wire frame; the final piece is 4.5 meters long and weighs more than one ton. Designed by industrial designer Yves Béhar, Waldemeyer conceived of the technological features, making the lighting wash across the surface in waves.

3
Moritz Waldemeyer
× Ron Arad for Swarovski
Lolita, 2004

Moritz Waldemeyer's series of multitudinous Swarovski lighting projects began at a time when he still worked for product and furniture designer Ron Arad. First was Lolita, a five-foot-tall spiraling chandelier, created for Swarovski's Crystal Palace Collection and later exhibited at the Venice Architecture Biennale and Tokyo Design Week. With over 1,000 white LEDs embedded into clear crystals and 31 micro-processors wired to a wooden ceiling plate, the high-tech lighting piece received text messages that scrolled down its face.

1
Moritz Waldemeyer
× Ron Arad for Swarovski
Miss Haze, 2005

Building on the success they had with the chandelier Lolita, Waldemeyer and Arad collaborated on Miss Haze, a rectangular piece bearing the fictional Lolita's last name. Arad's design incorporates 2,500 clear Swarovski crystals dangling on thin wires. Its lights, with electronics by Waldemeyer, were again controllable LEDs, allowing for motives to be reproduced on the chandelier and float on its wavelike surface. Programmed to function via a handheld personal digital assistant with a touchscreen, all kinds of shapes or letters could be drawn for Miss Haze to translate into tiny lucid pixels.

2

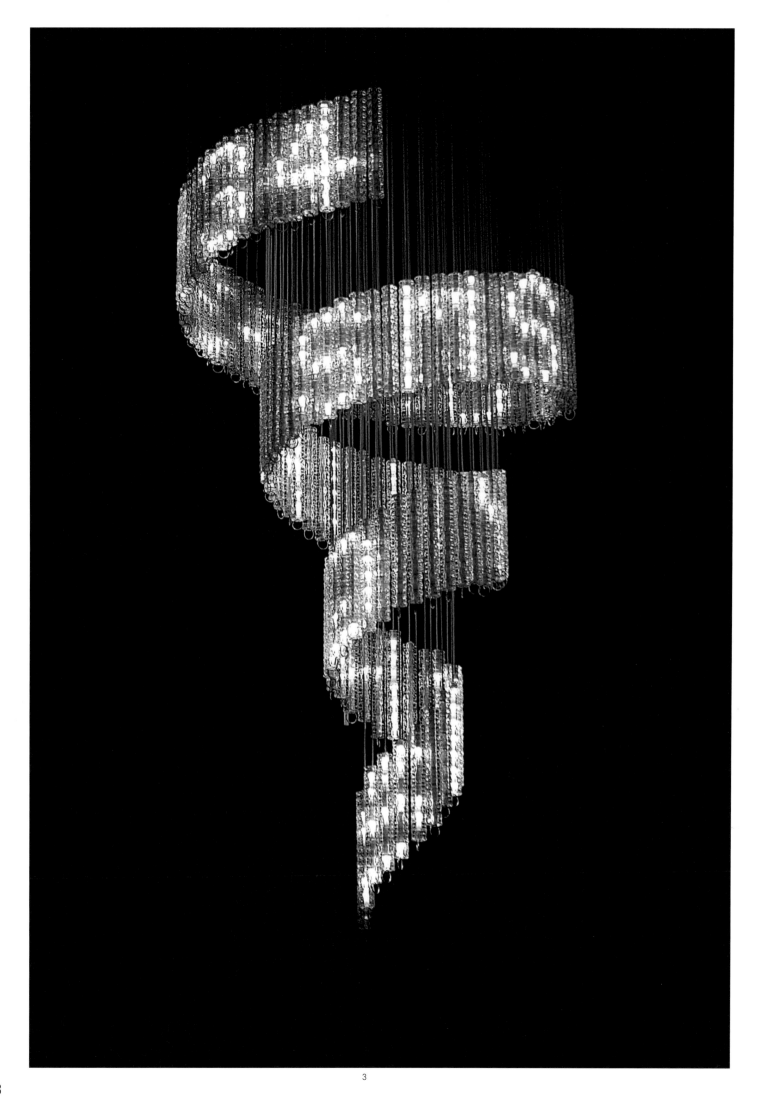

3

Moritz Waldemeyer for
ICA and Veuve Cliquot
Joyrider, 2008

Commissioned by the Institute of
Contemporary Arts and Veuve Cliquot,
Moritz Waldemeyer created Joyrider,
a set of two lighting accessories that
turns a bicycle into a moving light show.
An exercise in pure minimalism, each
light features just two LEDs, one fac-
ing each side. Clipped onto the wheel
spokes, the LEDs draw illuminated smi-
ley faces on rotating bicycle wheels.

Attached to two Veuve Cliquot colored prototype bikes designed by
Waldemeyer, the devices were sneak-
previewed at the Culture Show and then
auctioned at the ICA Figures of Speech
Charity Gala.

1

Fendi × Moritz Waldemeyer × Gibson
Les Paul Guitars, 2009

The collaboration of Silvia Venturini Fendi and the technologically-pioneering designer Moritz Waldemeyer stands for the amalgamation of craftsmanship, design and technological progress.

True to Fendi tradition, the leather lining of the guitars that the duo produced is handmade, with contrasting stitching typical of the "Selleria" collection. Waldemeyer then added LED illumination and lasers to the creation. Constructed for the Stereo Craft Design Performances at Design Miami 2009, the guitars were played live at the event by the American rock band OK Go, after being personalized with furs and laser lights to create real-time light graphics on a giant projection.

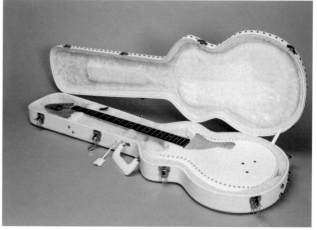

2

1

1
Matt W. Moore × Ray-Ban
Wayfarer Shades, 2010

Ray-Ban linked up with graphic artist Matt W. Moore on an exclusive line of hyper-geometric Wayfarers. The collection consists of three color schemes, one all-over pattern version, and two lo-fi alternatives with the graphic on the inside of the frames. A special artist advertisement was produced to celebrate the series of shades and Matt W. Moore's attractive signature style.

2
Matt W. Moore × Chiarelli Guitars
Rock N' Roll Series, 2010

Graphic artist Matt W. Moore and his friend James Chiarelli of Chiarelli Guitars got together in both Chiarelli's workshop and Moore's painting studio to work on three hand-painted Fender Telecasters and nine effects pedals. The guitars were completed with Fender standard series necks, Jason Lollar pickups, and vintage-style Fender hardware.

2

Damien Hirst × Flea for Other Criteria and the Silverlake Conservatory of Music
Multi-Colored Deluxe Spin Bass Guitar, 2011

This guitar was a unique charity collaboration between Damien Hirst and Flea, the bass player from The Red Hot Chili Peppers. It was produced in a limited total of 50 and packaged in a specially designed case including an "exquisite corpse" drawing by Hirst and Flea, as well as a framed monochrome butterfly gloss on canvas, a unique photograph of Hirst and Flea holding the guitar, and 20 specially-designed plectrums. Each piece is signed by Flea and Damien Hirst and has the edition number punched on the base of the neck and a custom Hirst-Flea logo on the headstock.

Produced and distributed by Other Criteria, the publishing and limited art edition company co-founded by Damien Hirst, all profits go to Flea's Silverlake Conservatory of Music, an organization that focuses on offering affordable or free music lessons and instruments to the youth of socially disadvantaged communities in the Los Angeles area.

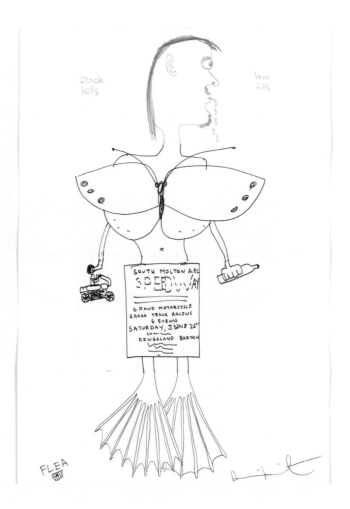

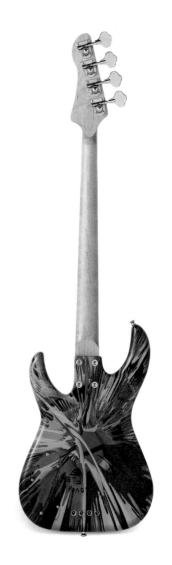

3

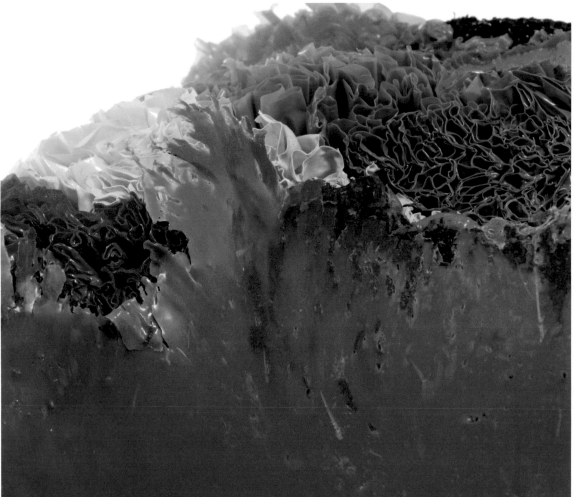

1
Tom Price
Meltdown Chair: PE Stripe, 2011

Tom Price's Meltdown Series is a collection of chairs that are all manufactured by means of a heated former, but using different materials. The latest of the series, the PE Stripe, is made by pressing the heated metal chair-shaped former into a stack of colorful woven plastic rugs. The chair's frame is made from solid stainless steel. Like all chairs in the Meltdown series, the PE Stripe is a one-off prototype.

2
Daniel Chadwick for Other Criteria
Backgammon Sets, 2011

Turning away from his sculptural installations for a moment, British artist Daniel Chadwick designed a range of signed and numbered limited-edition backgammon games. Available in four different color plans, the sets bring color and liveliness to a rainy Sunday afternoon. Produced in collaboration with and distributed by Other Criteria.

Photography: Other Criteria Ltd · © the artist

1

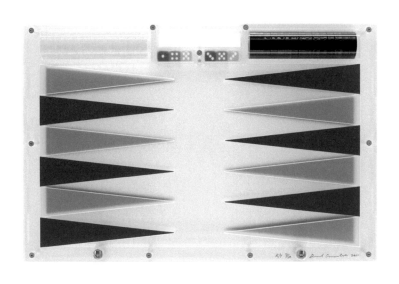

199

Jane Simpson for Other Criteria
Fresh Fresher, 2002

This edition of humorous silicone rubber kitchenware was created by British sculptor Jane Simpson. There are four versions of the set: a pair of jugs, a butter dish with butter knife, a meat tenderizer with lemon squeezer, and a shapely gravy boat. Each version is limited to 10 pieces and packaged in a specially-produced, cloth-covered, hinged book box including a copy of the publication Fresh Fresher. The set and book were produced with and for Other Criteria, the renowned art publisher and limited-edition producer co-founded by Damien Hirst.

Damien Hirst for Other Criteria
Pharmacy Ashrays, 2011

Three different styles of painted aluminum ashtrays were envisioned by British art icon Damien Hirst: "Lili U53," "3 Heads," and "Nicotine." These astrays were originally created for Pharmacy restaurant in Notting HIll, which the artist himself started together with public relations doyen Matthew Freud and restauranteur Jonathan Kennedy in 1997. After the much-celebrated venue closed its doors in 2003, most of the its interior accessories sold at Sotheby's for a total of £11,132,180. The ashtrays were not included in the auction, but reproduced and distributed by Other Criteria, another of Hirst's multitudinous projects.

1

Dror × Cappellini × Walt Disney
Tron Chair, 2010

An outright homage to the digital landscape of the Outlands terrain in Disney's science fiction saga, the Tron chair invites both fantasy and furniture enthusiasts to sit "off the grid." The jagged and angular raw data landscape of the movie inspired designer Dror Ben-shetrit to create an original sculptural armchair with complex intersecting layers. Working with varying textural surfaces and different shades of black, Dror managed to create a piece of furniture that is heavily reminiscent of digital rock. One-off hand-painted prototypes of the chair were on show at Design Miami 2010. To turn Dror's design into a finished product, Cappellini developed specific manufacture techniques to form the erratic peculiarities of the chair with a seamless finish and allow for large-scale production. Entirely made of recycled roto-molded plastic, the armchair has been produced for retail sale in a wide range of colors.

Jerome C. Rousseau for Walt Disney Signature
Quorra, 2011

Inspired by and custom designed for Disney's TRON: Legacy, Jerome Rousseau's futuristic sandal alludes to the silhouettes and structures of the futuristic world of the film. Made to be worn on set by the lead actress Olivia Wilde, a.k.a. Quorra, a golden and a pewter version of the limited edition five-inch platform heel were put on sale at the Tron Pop-Up Shop in Los Angeles, and then distributed via selected stores worldwide.

Known and admired for creating
conceptual footwear influenced by architecture, art, and industrialism, United Nude fascinated the fashion world
with the presentation of its second collaboration with Dutch designer Antoine
Peters as part of its 2010 spring/sum-
mer collection. Playing on the industry's excessive use of labels, the Label
Shoe's distinctive silhouette is com-
prised of a cluster of branded tags.

204

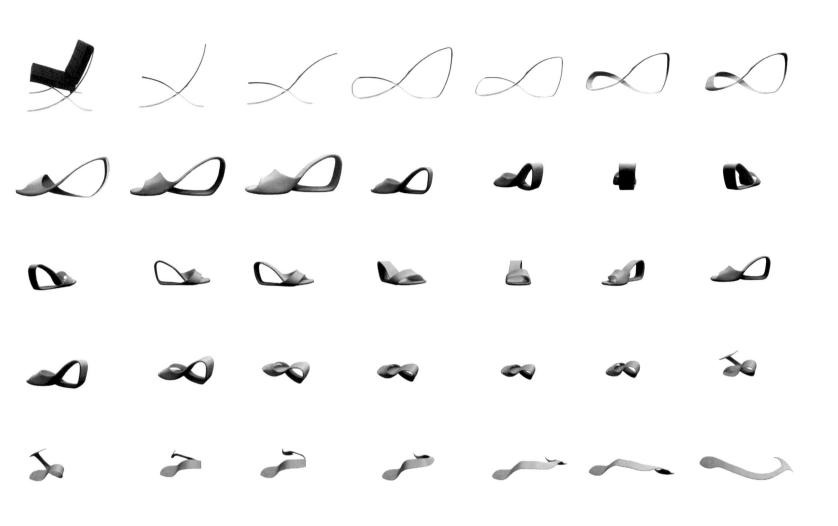

United Nude
Möbius, 2003

Co-founded by architect and design theorist Rem Koolhaas and the shoemaker Galahad Clark, United Nude launched its first creation, Möbius, in 2003, which has since become iconic in the world of design. Inspired by the concept of Mies van der Rohe's Barcelona Chair, the shoe was made of a single band uniting the sole, foot bed, and heel into one infinite piece—revolutionizing the traditional idea of heel construction.

1

1
Fendi × Abici
Amante Donna City Bike, 2009

Joining forces with the long-established Italian bicycle manufacturer Abici, Fendi fitted the Abici Amante Donna city bike with customized Selleria leather accessories. The result is a product of high-end craftsmanship that combines nostalgic style with high-tech features and luxurious lifestyle assets such as a GPS-navigator holder, a deluxe key and chain case, a bespoke pump, and a leather thermos cover. In place of an ordinary bike basket is a fully-accessorized trunk, reminiscent of a luxury beauty traveling case. Paying tribute to Fendi's traditional handicraft skills, all leather elements are cut, sewn, assembled, and embroidered by hand.

2
Pharrell Williams × Domeau & Pérès
Brooklyn Bike, 2010

After releasing the Perspective Chair in 2008, Pharrell Williams followed up on his collaboration with Domeau & Pérès, this time in an unprec- edented project called The Brooklyn Bike. Williams's passion for bikes used by New York's couriers led him to work on this model, which is fully wrapped in colored water buffalo leather. The monochrome leather cover contrasts with its white stitching. The bike was produced in France, in a limited edition of 12, to be offered to collectors and bike enthusiasts via the Domeau & Pérès showrooms and website.

Photography: Fred Dumur

3
Ilovedust for Tokyo Fixed Gear
Bespoke Track Bike, 2009

Ilovedust loves bikes, so the team jumped at the opportunity to work alongside technicians from Tokyo Fixed Gear in order to create a new bike for its London flagship store. Wrapping the super-light Figmo Stealth aluminum track frame with a bespoke all-over Ilovedust vinyl pattern, the collaborative group created a colorful edition for bike lovers and art lovers alike. The pink and orange design is paired with slick, black, carefully-chosen components.

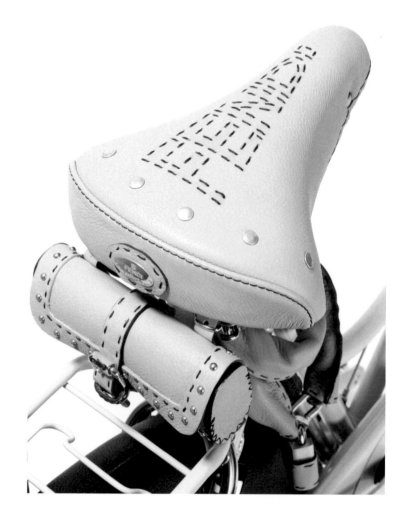

2

3

1
Super Motor
× Colette
Colette Super 50/100, 2011

Colette and the young Dutch Super Motor Company have teamed up to create a special limited edition version of the Super 50/100 motorcycle. A contemporary interpretation of the Honda Super Cub, the model is a semi automatic four-stroke, which is technically based on a so-called step-through motorcycle. Finished in Colette's distinctive blue and white, the Colette Super 50/100 was put on display and made available for sale at the famous Parisian department store.

2
Ilovedust for Yamaha
Giggle, 2009

By joining forces with Yamaha, Ilovedust designed a scooter with a bespoke narrative all-over pattern illustrating a trip that takes the viewer along canyons, past church spires and townhouses, across bridges, and into the countryside. Reflecting the cheerful spirit of the scooter as a mode of transportation, Ilovedust captured the scooter's essence by means of bright, distinct graphics and a bold overall style. The Giggle's aesthetic harks back to the 1960s with its analog components and bold bodywork. The scooter's new engine has far more horsepower than other models, and yet guarantees low emissions and petrol consumption.

The scooter comes with a classic 1971 helmet from Bell R/T with the new Ilovedust graphic.

1

2

Marc Newson for Riva
Aquariva by Marc Newson, 2010

Marc Newson partnered with long-established boat maker Riva and the brand's official designers, Officina Italiana Design, to reinterpret the Aquariva speedboat. An extension of the artist's work with planes and automobiles, Newson's design for the Aquariva vessel is a blend of form and function, unique in its conception and in its chosen materials. Its state-of-the-art nautical design pays tribute to La Dolce Vita of the 1950s and 1960s.

Upon the DNA of the original project created by Officina Italiana Design, which is in keeping with Riva's clas-

sic glamorous image, Newson introduced some innovative changes, such as the re-imagining of the transom (at the stern), the wrap-around, laminated glass windscreen, the split-cabin door entry, the increased functionality of the lounge and dining area, and the introduction of separate driver and passenger seats.

Launched as a limited edition of 22 in September 2010, The Aquariva by Marc Newson has been made available worldwide through Gagosian Gallery.

Photography: Jerome Kelagopian

Studio Job x Willem Nieland
Firmship 42, 2010

Antwerp-based Studio Job collaborated with Dutch nautical architect Willem Nieland to create Firmship 42, a contemporary artistic interpretation of centuries-old nautical traditions. The boat's forceful, bold, grey exterior, designed by nautical architect Willem Nieland, contrasts with the subtlety and welcoming warmth of Studio Job's interior work. Originally commissioned by the founder of the Moooi furniture brand, Casper Vissers, for his family's own use, the boat's refined interior has been crafted including every trick in the box, and of course with a loving attention to detail. Teak was used for the doors, the outdoor furniture, and the interior finish, reinforcing the boat's luxurious yet unobtrusive style.

Produced under the Firmship brand, this floating piece of art is available to order as a 12.8-meter boat. The next step will be the launch of a Firmship 60.

Photography: R. Kot

211

Marian Bantjes for Wallpaper*
Laser, 2010

Wallpaper* invited the publication's frequent contributor, Marian Bantjes, to design a boat for its 2010 Handmade edition. The Canadian graphic designer and illustrator delivered a graphically-enhanced Laser, one of the world's most popular sailboats, manufactured by LaserPerformance. Characterized by Bantjes's intricate ornamental style, the design references cubist patterns inspired by naval camouflage from the First and Second World Wars.

Produced in a limited edition of 12, the boat was made available to order from Laser. Performance Europe.

Photography: Benedict Redgrove

Exterior camouflage design by Jeff Koons.

PP. 213–215
Porfiristudio × Jeff Koons × Various Artists
Guilty, 2008

The "Guilty" is a project achieved through revolutionary boat architecture and an ideal example of high-class artist collaboration. Inspired by the idea of a floating living space, its structure is based on overlapping blocks organized vertically and horizontally around a path, with a focus on functionality and emotion. Calling the project the "ground zero" of yacht design, Milan-based Porfiristudio claim that the Guilty has given genesis to the development of possible new boat models. A significant part of their truly exceptional design concept is the incorporation of high class artworks—the external graphic painting by Jeff Koons certainly being the most distinguished one.

The graphic, almost bi-dimensional camouflage treatment came as the natural outcome of researching the ship's history, reference to a time when the technique of "escamotage" was used to hinder an enemy boat from understand-

Sarah Morris, <u>Guilty</u>, 1996. 101,6 × 152,4 cm, oil on canvas. Forward cabin.

ing a ship's type, size, distance, or direction. This technique remained efficacious until sonar and radar technology became available. The original "razzle dazzle" painting method was developed in large part by Koons, who attentively calibrated it for the boat's shape and size. Moreover, he improved it, introducing new elements by citing Lichtenstein on the sides, using an Iggy Pop effigy on the roof, and creating a three-dimensional effect from the aft view.

Apart from Koons's art intervention, the boat's interior includes artworks by some of the world's most renowned contemporary artists: on the lower deck, in the hull, the aft guest cabins are David Shrigley drawings, painted with a brush and black acrylic paint on board during the construction of the boat. In the other guest cabin is an artwork by Ricci Albenda entitled Eclipse, which functions according to anamorphosis. The soul of the boat is Sara Morris's Guilty painting in the VIP cabin. On the main deck, centered as a focal point of the main lounge, hangs an Anish Kapoor piece entitled Crate: a round concave dish built with several hexagonal mirror tiles, which reflect and reverse the surrounding space and views. The upper deck is an area of full outdoor view and seemingly limitless space. The inner walls are lined with mirror panels, reflecting the seascape's ceaseless glint. In this immaterial environment pulses and flicks Feelings, Martin Creed's neon tube piece.

Design Concept: Ivana Porfiri Photography: Andrea Ferrari

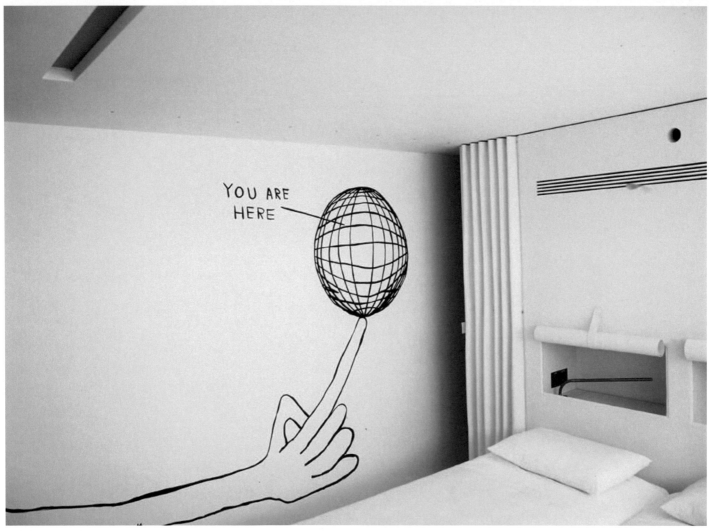

David Shrigley, <u>Untitled</u>, 2008. Variable dimensions Wall painting. Port side cabin.

Art Work by: Anish Kapoor, <u>Hex Mirror</u>, 2008. 120 x 120 x 45.7 cm polished stainless steel. Lounge.

Hayon Studio for Bisazza
Jet Set, 2008

Experimenting with the potential use of Bisazza's materials, Hayon Studio created a humorous installation to be presented at the Milan Furniture Fair 2008. Built of fiber and silver Bisazza mosaic tiles, with a cabin of crystal and wings of leather, the full-size vintage-style plane appears luxurious and surreal. Precise stage lighting adds to the overall theatrical atmosphere of the installation, which could certainly be part of a scene from an old Hollywood movie.

Photography: Nienke Klunder

Adventures

Brand Experience—
Becoming Part of The Story

4

Constantly bombarded with information, the modern consumer has become more selective and increasingly resistant to conventional sales messages. In recognition of these changes, and with the understanding that joint adventures keep relationships alive—sometimes forming unbreakable bonds—many marketing departments appear to be modeling communication strategies at the intersection between the brand's capabilities and everyday life to create marketing projects that consumers will love.

Brand experience grants admission, forges opportunities for participation, and evokes a feel-

1

2

ing of togetherness. More interactive than meditative, brand experiences can create situations that are relevant and inspiring. Some of these fascinate us with fabulous ceremony, such as Fiona Leahy's ^{PP. 278–279} dinner party installation for Stella McCartney. Others entertain us with crackpot activities like paddling over poison-green jelly lakes upon Selfridge's roof, as was the case in Bompas & Parr's ^{P. 261} Voyage of Discovery created for the sweetener company Truvia. The narrative coffee table in Iittala's Story of a Mug café ^{1 | PP. 254–255} invites us to study and review bygone decades, and …,staat's ^{PP. 246–247} perfectly orchestrated House of Bols is assured to beguile our senses. At best, brand experience communicates not only ambition, but also the personal benefits of association.

In various ways, the events compiled in this section represent phenomena of social and behavioral relevance. And further, they reflect the best efforts of contemporary inquiry into corporate identity and communication. Taking a proactive stand amid the modern information deluge, experience-based projects refine the vision of branding and present it as an energetic medium rather than a mere vehicle for information. As such, and in view of the plethora of choices, these experiential endeavors may be among the most responsible, if indeed least calculable activities of brand marketing.

Compared with the other three categories in this book, the examples of adventurous brand experience in this chapter represent the communication mode least encumbered by marketing precedents. The least professionalized category, it may stand out as the most compelling yet most perilous. But precariousness is what can lead marketers to depend on generic situations that eventually become indistinguishable from other promotional events, and public participation runs the risk of degenerating into routine indifference.

The best brand events make their visitors live to see, or even better, to do things that are worth telling friends about later. Among various unbelievable and essentially extraordinary things,

3

unpredictable ones are likely to be the most thrilling. Therefore, projects that appear to build on the momentum of a spontaneous, virtuous, and self-reinforcing process promise to be particularly effective.

If there's anything that a successful brand event seems to loathe, it is stringency, dogmatism, and the acceptance of a fixed set of rules. But however spontaneous some may seem, however game-like, ritualistic, or purely contemplative, the brand event is certainly a purposeful activity. Purpose implies precision and therefore necessitates meticulous strategical planning. Bompas & Parr say that they do indeed script a lot of seemingly visitor-generated "spontaneous" moments into their projects, to induce or bring forward certain situations out of countless options. For the Truvia Voyage of Discovery event they designed, Bompas & Parr had an elevator filled with books for visitors to steal. 3 | P. 261 Loads got taken (and secretly replaced) across the installation, leaving the visitor with the thrill of the illicit.

But however strategically planned and based on a distinct set of skillfully-composed characteristics, the brand event never wanders far from everyday life: its success depends on many random contingency factors, and is therefore almost impossible to calculate in advance. Often the design's implementation demands on a leap of faith. The notion of adventure may thus be shared by those in charge and, in this context, the denotation of the term may be rather negative.

The successful brand event, however, will certainly reward the believer with a sense of consequence: its participants will become brand ambassadors, spreading the message that will potentially manifest in news stories, blog entries, and occasional amateur snapshots. As such, the aura of the actual event continues to breath just beyond the recipient's immediate grasp.

Designed for a brief life, events resist the threat of being turned into sterilized objects of remote aesthetic appreciation. They rarely become overexposed, rather, they succeed in escaping the inevitable death-by-publicity to which many other means of promotion are condemned. Presenting themselves in disposable terms, they literally die right after they have happened, just before the mass media has a chance to absorb and conserve them, leaving behind nothing but a mythical resonance that does not disown its origin. Soon (almost immediately), they become a "somewhere," a "some time ago," and may even become precious. It is this game of planned obsolescence and such taking part in the action that counts. The successful brand experience goes full circle from an aspirational promise to a haunting memory.

New York-based luxury specialty retailer Barneys linked up with the House of Gaga to host Gaga's Workshop: Barneys' 2011 Holiday campaign and Lady Gaga's interpretation of Santa's legendary workshop.

The unique collaboration occupied an entire floor of the Barneys Madison Avenue flagship store, and brought together renowned creative talents including Lady Gaga, fashion director Nicola Formichetti, and artists Eli Sudbrack and Christophe Hamaide-Pierson of Assume Vivid Astro Focus (avaf). Known for their visually spectacular and multimedia installations, the avaf duo—working with the Barneys team under the creative direction of Dennis Freedman—developed the signature style for Gaga's Workshop, which was carried through the workshop itself all the way to the store's windows, as well as through the various materials and products created in conjunction with this project. Working closely with Lady Gaga under the creative direction of Nicola Formichetti, Barneys produced a range of exclusive limited-edition small gift products made available for a limited time at Gaga's Workshop. In the spirit of the holiday season, 25% of sales from all items featured in Gaga's Workshop went to a charity of Lady Gaga's choice.

Creative director of Barneys New York: Dennis Freedman × Photography: Tom Sibley

Artek × Tobias Rehberger
Was du liebst, bringt dich auch zum Weinen, 2009

In close collaboration with the Finnish furniture designers at Artek, German artist Tobias Rehberger created the cafeteria for the pavilion at the 2009 Venice Biennale. His design makes use of customized Artek furniture, and is based on a complex scheme of geometric forms with contrasting colors. Bearing reference to the "razzle dazzle" or "dazzle painting" style used on ships during the First World War to disorient the enemy, the space entitled Was du liebst, bringt dich auch zum Weinen ("What you love will bring you to wine") became a visually bewildering but certainly unique environment, bringing Tobias Rehberger the Golden Lion as best artist at the 53rd Biennale di Venezia.

Photography: Wolfgang Guenzel

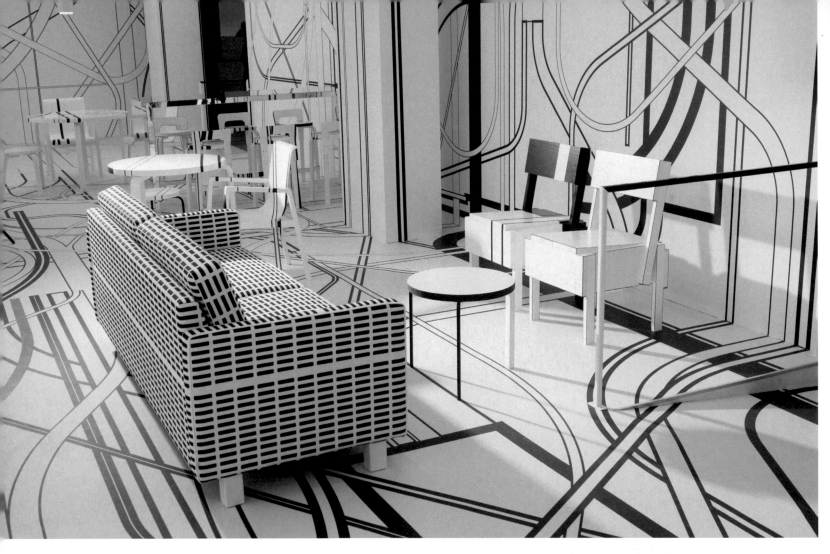

Artek x Tobias Rehberger
Nothing Happens for a Reason, 2010

A follow-up to their earlier collaboration on the occasion of the Venice Art Biennale 2009, German artist Tobias Rehberger teamed up with Finnish furniture design firm Artek to develop a creative space installed at the Logomo Café in in Turku, Finland. Enitled Nothing Happens for a Reason, the project tied in with the abstract, disorienting battle ship aesthetic of the previous Venice space and the geometrical complexity typical for Rehbergers's work in general. Essentially a white space with lines drawn through it regardless of any physical obstructions, the only color to be spotted in the space is an orange Artek lamp.

Photography: Bo Stranden

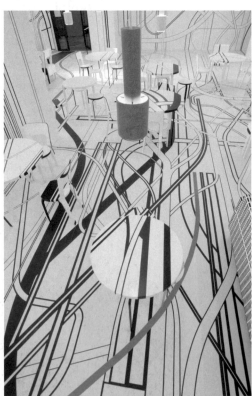

Rafael de Cárdenas (Architecture At Large) for OHWOW and Cappellini
OHWOW at Cappellini, 2010/2011

Architect and designer Rafael de Cárdenas partnered with Al Moran and Aaron Bondaroff of OHWOW to create a festive pop-up shop in Cappellini's flagship showroom on Wooster Street in So-Ho—the second OHWOW venue in New York following the OHWOW Book Club on Waverly Place in the West Village. Consistent with the signature graphic design aesthetic of de Cárdenas, the pop-up shop relied on bold lines, color and contrast, plus a certain candy cane and gift wrap aesthetic, immersing customers in a kaleidoscope-like scene of brightly-colored, crisscrossing translucent bands to ultimately create the sensation of being inside an oversized gift. Cappellini's chairs, guised in colorful wrapping, served as pedestals for OHWOW publications on display.

Design Team: Rafael de Cárdenas, Justin Capuco, Robert Passov, Scott Rominger, Sam Sutcliffe   Photography: floto + warner

Byggstudio for
Crystal Gallery
Crystal Magic Box - Portable Gallery, 2009

Byggstudio designed Crystal Magic Boxes, a series of portable trunks, for the Stockholm-based gallery Crystal. Opening up like a magician's box, the trunks are used for art fair stands and temporary exhibitions abroad, functioning both as display shelves for the gallery's art objects and as shipping containers. Custom sticky tape for packing matches the orange and pink leather straps of the trunks to make a complete and beautiful package.

Photography: Jun-Hi Wennergren Nordling

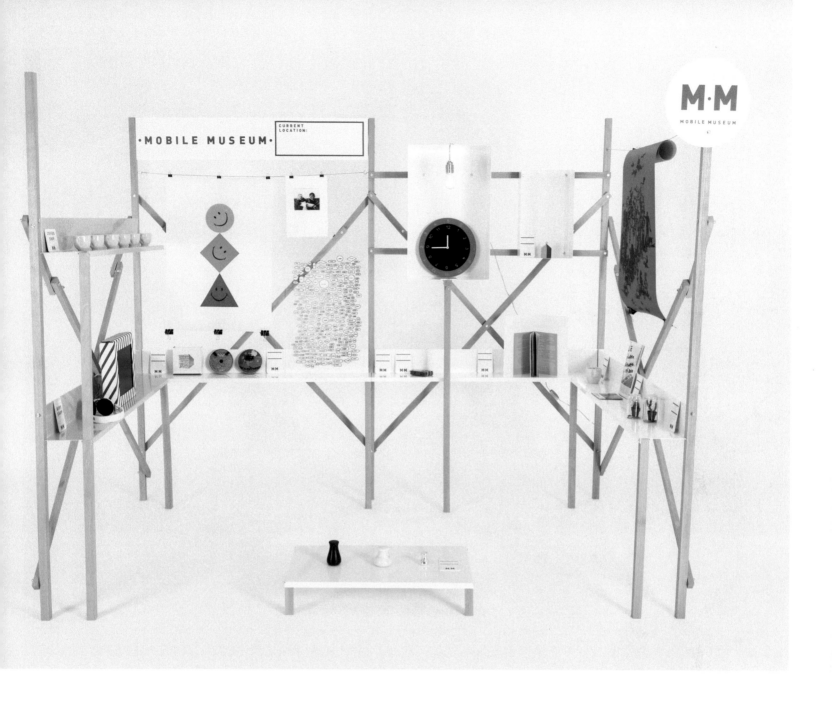

Fabrica
The Mobile Museum, 2011

Brought into being by Fabrica, the Benetton Group's communication research center, The Mobile Museum is a changing collection of works by creatives of different disciplines from all over the world. Artists, designers, illustrators, photographers, and a wide range of practitioners have been invited to contribute anything from small ephemeral printed material to found objects, photographs, small sculptures, industrial products, posters, postcards, sketches, and digital projects. This traveling exhibit evolves depending on its location, allowing the location itself to dictate the theme.

Designed by Fabrica's designers Philip Bone and Dean Brown, the first Mobile Museum exhibition took place during the Milan Furniture Fair 2011, under the curatorial theme of "family." The second MM exhibition was staged at the Victoria and Albert Museum as part of the Friday Late Summer Camp program, and most recently it was shown in Brussels as part of Design September 2011.

Over the course of its three events, The Mobile Museum has received and exhibited works from various famous contributors, such as Stefan Sagmeister, Timorous Beasties, Jean Marc Gady, Kiki Van Eijk, Studio Makkink & Bey, Sam Baron, Mind Design and Inventory Studio.

All donations are photographed and archived to be viewed online (www.themobilemuseum.net), and as part of the museum's growing permanent collection.

Designers: Philip Bone & Dean Brown
Creative Director: Sam Baron   Photography: Gustavo Millon

1

Nymphenburg
× Saâdane Afif
× RaebervonStenglin
The Fairytale Recordings, 2011

Traditional German porcelain manufacturer Nymphenburg, renowned for handicraft artistry and celebrated collaborations with contemporary designers and artists, decided to partner with French performance artist Saâdane Afif and Zurich-based gallery RaebervonStenglin in an exceptional interdisciplinary project. The Fairytale Recordings venture was based upon a revision of Afif's earlier works, song texts that various writers and artists developed to reflect the nature of his projects, and upon a performance with opera singer and actress Katharina Schrade in which each of these texts was spoken or acted out. Reinterpreted to form a new composite verse, the verbal material was recorded as a voice-over and then sealed in a specially crafted Nymphenburg vase.

Eight such vases were handmade in the Nymphenburg Porcelain Manufactory master workshops, each vase portraying a different position or moment in time from Katharina Schrade's performance.

Presented in the Schinkel Pavillon in Berlin, the project was played out in its entirety, featuring Schrade's performance in eight vases.

Performance view: Schinkel Pavillon, Berlin Photo: Jan Windszus[1] Courtesy: Galerie Mehdi Chouakri, Berlin, RaebervonStenglin, Zurich

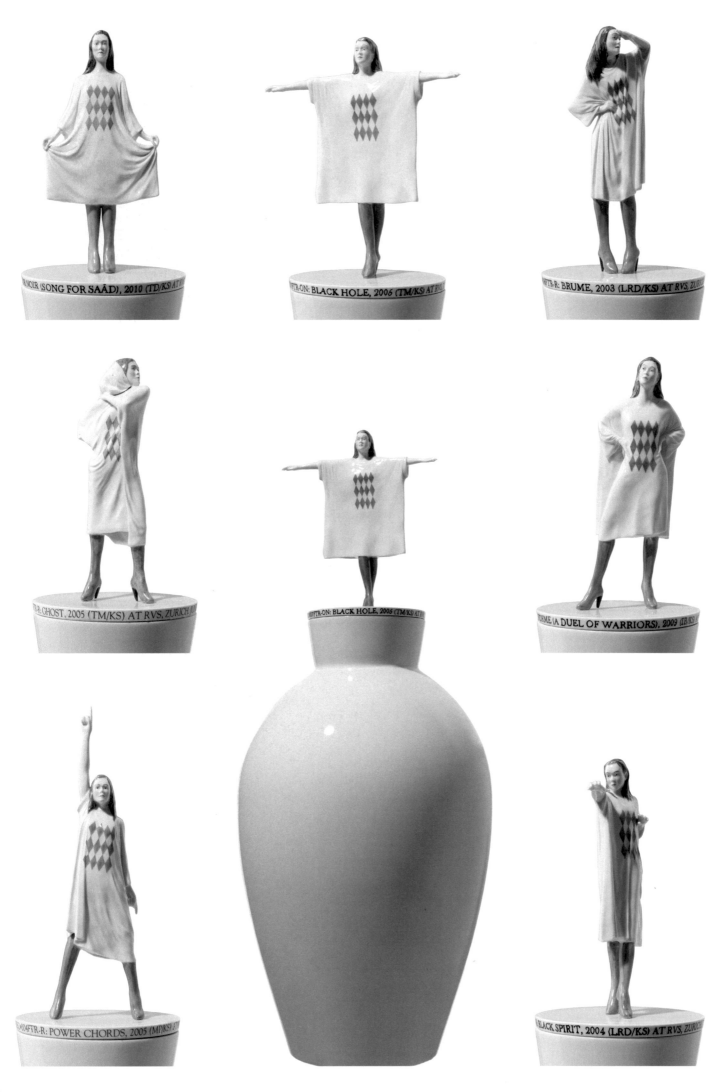

R NOIR (SONG FOR SAÁD), 2010 (TD/KS) AT R

FTR-ON: BLACK HOLE, 2005 (TM/KS) AT RV

FTR-R: BRUME, 2003 (LRD/KS) AT RVS, ZURICH

R: GHOST, 2005 (TM/KS) AT RVS, ZURICH

FTR-ON: BLACK HOLE, 2005 (TM/KS) AT

ORME (A DUEL OF WARRIORS), 2009 (IB/KS)

04FTR-R: POWER CHORDS, 2005 (MP/KS)

BLACK SPIRIT, 2004 (LRD/KS) AT RVS, ZURICH

Yuri Suzuki for Red Stripe
Make Something from Nothing, 2011

Red Stripe launched its "Make" campaign, a series of cultural projects celebrating the DIY culture of the brand's Jamaican roots, with Yuri Suzuki's Make Something from Nothing endeavor.

The London-based designer and sound artist, who is famous for his homemade music machines, constructed the specially-commissioned audio installation with the help of designer Matthew Kneebone using thousands of Red Stripe cans—many of them collected at Notting Hill Carnival. The fully functioning sound sculpture, which draws inspiration from bass-heavy Jamaican sound systems, was put on show at Village Underground, an emerging gallery and project space in Shoreditch, where it was played live in an exclusive DJ set.

Photography: Ed Aves[1], Guy Archard[2]

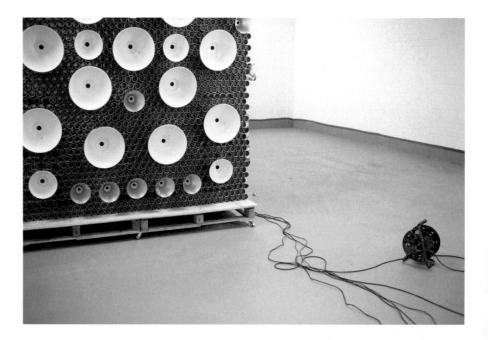

1

2

Hayon Studio for Bisazza
Tournament Installation, 2009

For Italian luxury design brand Bisazza, Hayon Studio created The Tournament, an installation resembling a gigantic chess set, with two-meter-high ceramic chess pieces on a custom-made Bisazza mosaic glass chess board. For the 32 handcrafted chess pieces, Hayon collaborated with the Italian ceramics experts at Bosa.

Each piece is unique and hand-painted by Jamie Hayon. The Tournament bears reference to the historical city of London and The Battle of Trafalgar, which was organized like a chess game of naval strategy. Many of the chess pieces are inspired by iconic London buildings, citing their domes, towers, and spires in Hayon's very personal style. The Tournament was launched at London Design Festival 2009.

Photography: Nienke Klunder

234

as well as actual Dyson machine parts into his collection.

As a result, Issey Miyake pioneered the award-winning A-POC (a piece of cloth) process, which allows for the computerized production of continuous tubes of fabric in particular shapes and patterns. Bringing the collaboration full circle, Dyson dedicated the 2007 version of the Dyson DC16 handheld cleaner to Issey Miyake

Designers: Sir James Dyson and Dai Fujiwara

PP. 236–239
Dyson × Issey Miyake
Catwalk Show, Clothing Range and DC16 Handheld Cleaner, 2007

Vacuum cleaners and high fashion don't have much in common. This unusual collaboration began with Issey Miyake's head of design, Dai Fujiwara, visiting Dyson's Research Design and Development center in Wiltshire, UK, and posing Sir James Dyson the challenge of bringing wind power to his catwalk show. Dyson, who had admired Issey Miyake's bold approach to design ever since seeing Miyake's 1985 solo exhibition in London, decided to introduce giant yellow hoses to the catwalk. Commonly used for police dog training or to extract exhaust fumes from aircrafts, the tubes were tested in a huge warehouse at Dyson's RDD Center in the UK before being flown out for further testing in France, with the aim of bringing a wave of fresh air to Issey Miyake's runway at Paris Fashion Week.

In continuation of the fruitful partnership, Dai Fujiwara began incorporating blueprints from Dyson designs

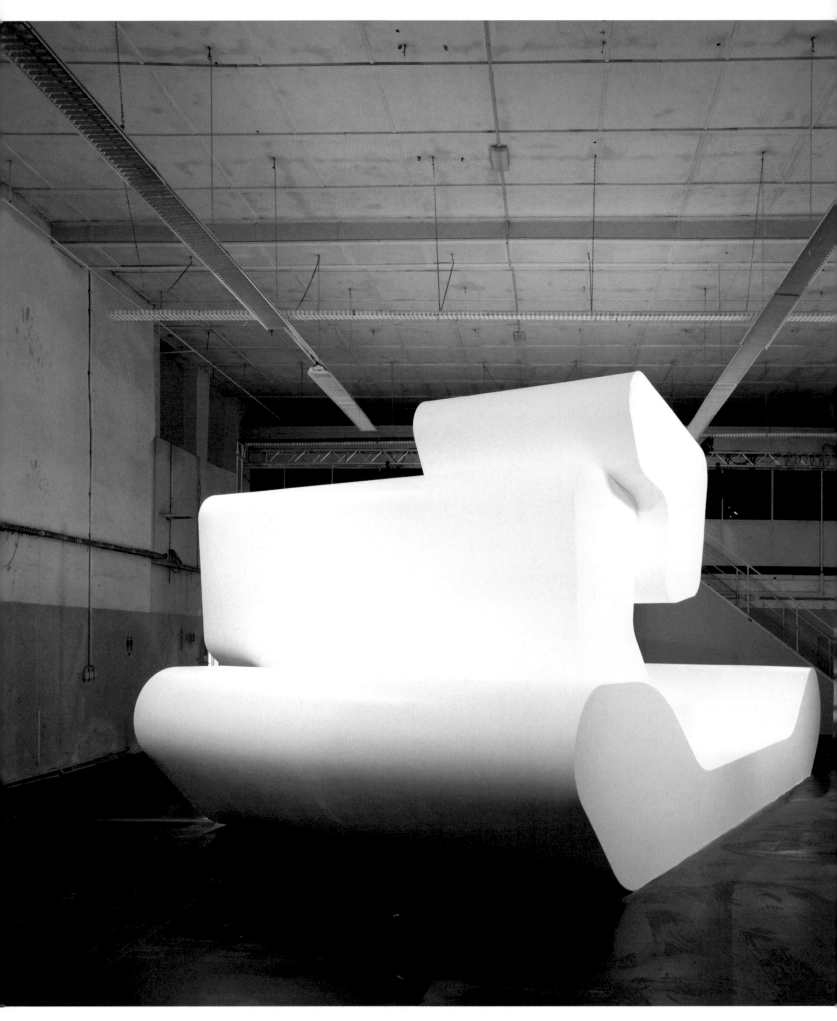

J. MAYER H. Architects
for Calvin Klein
Multi-Brand Event in Berlin

This event presented the Spring 2011 and Resort 2011 offerings which were showcased within the context of a special installation piece created by prominent Berlin-based, J. MAYER H. Architects. The architecture office was commissioned by Calvin Klein to create a unique and impactful experience that unites its various lines under an overall theme and concept to express a total lifestyle statement. This event was another in a series of global events that Calvin Klein, Inc. has held over the past few years in important and exciting global markets such as London, Milan, Tokyo, Singapore, Shanghai, Sydney, Seoul, Dubai, Rio de Janeiro, Los Angeles, and New York.

1

Moritz Waldemeyer × Hussein Chalayan
Readings (Laser Dresses), 2007

Spurred by his urge for technological experimentation, British-Turkish fashion designer Hussein Chalayan created his collection Readings with the help of electrical designer Moritz Waldemeyer.

Inspired by themes of ancient sun worship and the contemporary phenomenon of celebrity, the collaboration brought about a series of boldly shaped dresses from which laser beams radiated. The haunting play of light that represented the relationship between audience and icon was enhanced by Swarovski crystals that, applied to the fabric, either took in or deflected the lasers depending on their angle.

Hundreds of lasers were integrated into each piece, attached by custom-designed, servo-driven brass hinges, allowing for the lasers to move

and for the pieces of the collection to become ephemeral forms of perpetual change.

Matching the technological features of the collection, Hussein Chalayan unveiled Readings on-screen with a film by Nick Knight and Ruth Hogben, side-stepping the conventional runway setup.

1

Moritz Waldemeyer
× Hussein Chalayan
Airborne (Video Dresses), 2007

Teaming up with light specialist Moritz Waldemeyer to realize the out-

landish concept of his video dresses, fashion designer Hussein Chalayan presented his collection of LED-based moving pieces as part of his spring/summer 2007 show in Paris.

Based on off-the-shelf components, standard manufacturing techniques, and about 15,000 LEDs embedded in the fabric, each piece is one of a kind. One piece displays hazy silhouettes of sharks in the sea, another a time-lapsed sequence of a rose opening and closing. A layer of loose white fabric covers the LEDS to blur and distort the images and create an effect of mesmerizing ambiguity.

2

3
Moritz Waldemeyer
× Hussein Chalayan
111 (Robotic Dresses), 2006

Taking the transient nature of fashion and the many trends that evolved throughout the last century as the subject of his spring/summer 2007 collection, Hussein Chalayan created six pieces that transform themselves to magically morph through decades of changing fashions.

The transformation is subtle, achieved through fluid movements of raveling and unraveling, zipping up and tearing open. It all happens as if by magic—each piece seems alive, gently unfolding like the petals of a flower: a high-necked Victorian gown frees itself from its own chastity, the top splitting open and the hemline retreating to transmute into a crystal-embellished flapper dress.

The magic was made possible by Moritz Waldemeyer's engineering skills. After six months of experimenting with servo-driven motors, pulleys, and wires, the lighting designer mastered the challenge of keeping the integrated technology lightweight yet strong enough to maneuver different fabrics and materials and bring Hussein Chalayan's progressive tailoring to life.

3

Fabio Novembre
for Philips
Post Digital, 2007

For Transitions, an initiative for creative architectural lighting solution by Philips Electronics, Milan-based interior architect Fabio Novembre created an interactive walk-in light installation. The piece was inspired by the designer's aim to create a relationship between the digital and the human, expressed through the relation of the grid of LEDs to the movement of a body in space.

Photography: Pasquale Formisano

The Macallan × Roja Dove
Aroma Box, 2011

Working together with the perfumery Roja Dove, The Macallan created a magical box of aroma oils to be used by its brand team and global ambassadors for presentation. The kit contains 12 unique natural oil blends. The first six scents showcase some common characteristics of whisky, arranged in pairs of opposites to intrigue and educate about the power of aroma, while the second six represent Roja's interpretation of the essential sensory character of The Macallan. Roja Dove selected the finest natural ingredients for The Macallan aroma oils: for example, the Rose de Mai, from Grasse, requires over 300,000 hand-picked roses to make one kilo of oil. The box that houses the twelve oils is made of oak wood from The Macallan estate and manufactured by Duke Christie, a highly-skilled cabinet maker who lives close to The Macallan.

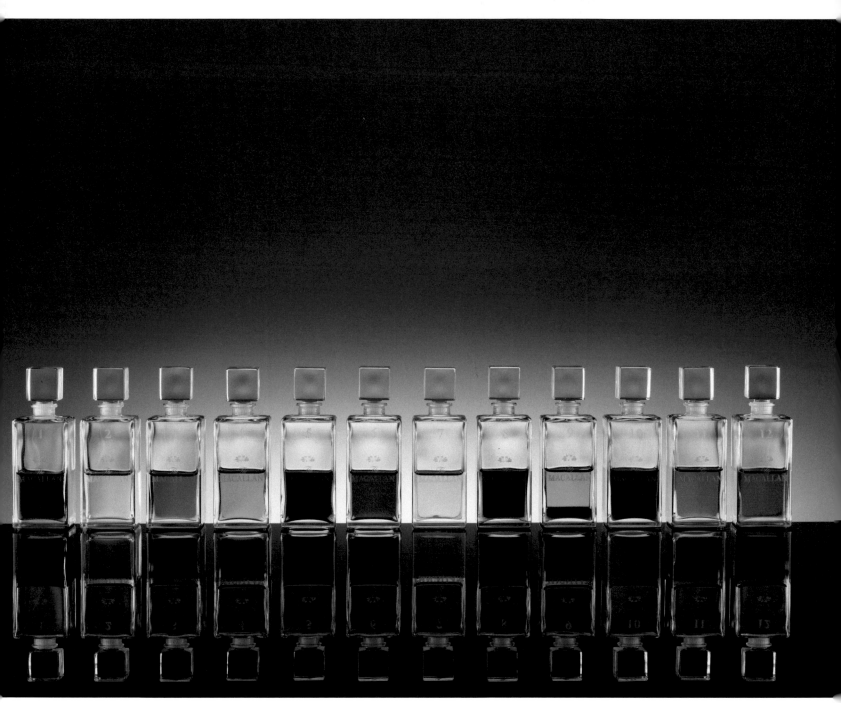

...,staat for Bols
House of Bols, 2007

After returning to Amsterdam, the city where his ancestors set up the company in 1575, Lucas Bols chose creative agency ...,staat to develop an adventure land of jenevers and liqueurs that would bring Bols products into contemporary light. Understanding that communication has many forms, ...,staat created an experience that cannot be categorized as either museum or brand attraction. Striking colors, spherical lighting, and specific materials amount to an unexpected, daring, and particularly immersive ambiance. Occupying 17 unique rooms in two stories, the House of Bols featured The Hall of Taste, an eruption of colors and smells, where visitors are invited to test their taste buds, savoring a great range of aromatic products, The Mirror Bar, a cocktail bar in a square room made entirely out of mirrors, The Flair Booth, where guests could train to become top bartenders, tape their experiences and email it to their friends, The World of Cocktails, a 280-degree projected music video experience with a customized soundtrack, and the Delft Blue Room, an exhibition of the famous BOLS/KLM houses containing Bols liqueurs and jenevers.

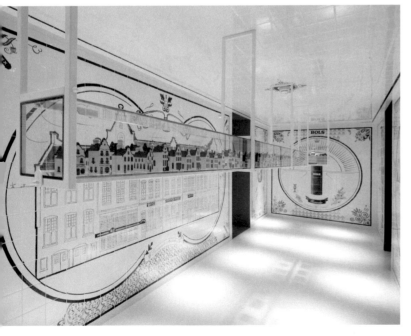

In the redesigned Deutsche Bank headquarters in Frankfurt, the Brand-Space, a collaborative project of ART+COM and Coordination Berlin, provides insight into the bank's history, its present identity, and its brand philosophy. The Deutsche Bank logo, a radically reductive 1970s design by Anton Stankowski, was the starting point for the space's design. Through a method called anamorphosis, a flat shape can

be translated into a three-dimensional structure that is legible as a whole from only one vantage point. Based on the concept of anamorphosis, ART+COM and Coordination Berlin developed several complex anamorphic sculptures from the Deutsche Bank logo, in order to form a series of interactive, reactive, and auto-active installations—all visually linked by guilloché, the intricate pattern of lines usually found on banknotes.

LOVE for Johnnie Walker
Johnnie Walker House, 2011

Entrusted with the task of familiarizing Chinese consumers with the culture and heritage of Scotch whisky, Manchester-based brand agency LOVE conceived of the Johnnie Walker House. LOVE teamed up with Shanghai-based interior designers Asylum to realize the concept of an experiential brand space. The result features a variety of installations, such as a copper sculpture that demonstrates the whisky distillery process, and an interactive blending table that invites special guests into a journey of discovery through the history of Johnnie Walker whisky.

Commissioned by LOVE to trigger "whisky conversations," London-based illustrator Chris Martin of TOY designed a series of commemorative porcelain whisky bottles that depict Johnnie Walker's epic journey from Scotland to China over a hundred years ago. Each of the Chinese-style bottles features a different part of the story, so that when lined up, the series reveals the whole sequence. Selecting Martin's illustration as a key visual for the location, LOVE adapted it for the interior decoration of the space as well as for use on marketing material.

...,staat for Hendrick's Gin
Hendrick's Glorious Curiosities Cocktail Lab

Under the creative lead of ...,staat, Hendrick's gin took over the Amsterdam venue Brug9. The custom-made bar installation entitled Glorious Curiosities Cocktail Laboratory was inspired by Hendrick's Curiositorium, which references the Victorian era of inventions and embraces refined ingredients such as the glorious Dutch cucumber and the Bulgarian rose petal. For two days only, guests were invited to experience Hendrick's Victorian gin in a truly marvelous setting, gracefully attended to by "shaker boys" and "grace girls," who offered drinks and style advice on how to become a modern dandy.

Byggstudio for Iittala
The Story of a Mug, 2010

The Story of a Mug is a book exploring the origins of the Iittala Teema mug. On the basis of Iittala's factory notes and mug pattern sketches, Byggstudio designed a very personal artifact to be released in October 2010 by Everyday Life Books, Apartamento magazine, and Iittala.

An important part of the book's story was a pop-up café in Stockholm that opened its doors for three days in December 2010 to launch and market the release of the book. Hosted by Byggstudio and Apartamento magazine, the café brought the themes and objects presented in the book to life. Designed as a schematic timeline, the café table creates a time travel experience through the history of Iittala's product design and coffee culture; cups, saucers, jugs, and sugar bowls were arranged in accordance with the customs of each period in time represented; cakes, coffee, sugar and milk were also arranged according to the style of each period. A custom-built bar inspired by café interiors of the 1700s complemented the historical coffee experience.

Photography: Lotten Pålsson

The table worked as a schematic timeline, from 1700-2010. The guests were welcome to sit down and experience different style periods, coffees, and cakes. The timeline idea related to the historic facts in a playful way and offered an interactive and genuine experience through tasting, learning, and seeing. The table was set with cups, saucers, jugs, and sugar bowls authentic to each period in time. The cakes, coffee, sugar, and milk also followed the customs of that time. Historical mug and coffee facts were integrated in the interior setting by the tablecloth print and paper napkins with texts.

THE STORY

OF A MUG

The mug is perhaps one of the most used and loved objects in our cupboards. The Story of a Mug explores the narratives that unexpectedly lie behind this unassuming object. This book was originally published in Swedish as part of Iittala's Local Mug Initiative, launched in 2008.

Book exploring the origins of the Iittala Teema mug.

The Factory Notes Mug

The bar, custom-built for the occasion, wasinspired by the interiors of old coffee salons from the 1700s.

Visitors drinking coffee from the saucer—the old fashioned way.

1

After Bompas & Parr began as a jelly company making wobbly versions of St. Paul's Cathedral, Sam Bompas and Harry Parr are now among "the 15 people who will define the future of arts in Britain," according to The Independent. The fact is that within a month of founding the company, the duo were hosting full 12-course Victorian breakfasts—and they have continued expanding their horizons and ambitions quite remarkably ever since. They manage to continue coming up with fantastic ideas, by reading old and arcane books, for example, and by spending a good deal of time in the pub together. The difference between theirs and most other people's pub inventions is that Bompas & Parr are committed enough to spend the next six months making their ideas happen.

In doing so, they work as artists, chefs, architects, photographers, and even magicians. They don't care much what people call them, as long as the work is strong. With the skill and will of royal jesters on the court of marketing, they are in fact total outsiders to such a world. Ideas that university programs teach aspiring advertising students come to Bompas & Parr quite naturally: "If an idea needs any more than a few words to be explained, it's probably rubbish. This is why we don't try hard on pitches. If you have to sell an idea, it's probably not worth doing." Typically zapped to the potential client in an email, any project's central idea needs to work naturally for the brand and communicate its story in a thrilling, but credible way.

but also the personal and social benefits of association.

Jelly and booze seem to be enough to make a memorable experience and put a smile on anyone's face—but it's not as easy as that. Most of Bompas & Parr's projects are based on a ton of research, which is why they are registered as a chemical research lab and possess a bewildering array of chemicals. These materials range from powders that will ignite when champagne is poured on them to industrial crystal kits and bioluminescent enzymes. For any given installation or meal, the two will work with neuroscientists, mixologists, inorganic chemists, astronomers, astrologers, animal trainers, engineers, food technologists, and woodsmen. To carry something off with aplomb certainly takes a lot of craft. Maybe that is why strangers trust Bompas & Parr enough to eat some fairly weird stuff. And most clients seem to trust them, too.

The best clients are those "who understand what they're good at and what we're good at. When doing the sorts of ambitious projects we work on, it helps if they are a swashbuckler too. Working with Truvia was unbelievable. The realized that they couldn't be beat at bringing product to market, but trusted us to create a spectacular brand experience. This trust meant we were able to focus on what we're good at, delivering an epic installation rather than spending time explaining what's happening and defending the creative process. They were magic to work with."

Despite all faith, some project ideas are just too far out to be realized. They once had a plan for a castle with medieval metal bands, medieval kebabs, live snakes in the toilets, explosions, and ether cocktails. "The line was

"Good work is a bit like pornography—hard to describe, but you know it when you see it."

Branding works a bit like storytelling: The brand itself represents the content of the narrative, its marketers are constantly on the lookout for new and engaging ways to tell it. Outplaying mascots, testimonials and celebrity brand ambassadors, Bompas & Parr offer a different narrative mode, another set of methods, to communicate the content. Instead of pitching, spotlighting, and extolling the virtue of a product, they experiment with it in order to create interplay, experience, and eventually a cherished memory. As such, their concepts communicate not only ambition,

drawn at child mixologists—though there were two lined up who had savage repertoires." Sometime in the future, they would like to "bring an entire iceberg to New York City to use in cocktails." They insist that they have figured out the technique for doing this, and that they've established with a physicist that this can be 1000 times more energy-efficiently than making ice using an ice machine.

But why ponder about future projects? The ones at hand celebrate the magic of the moment, put smiles on faces, and thereby buy time in people's brains. "Compare this to the two seconds brands have to appeal to people's attention as they walk past the product in the supermarket. Or the thirty seconds they have when people watch their expensive ads on TV. As we have consumers for an hour or more, we can tell them really nuanced and complex stories." These are adventure stories, set in unchartered worlds that we are dying to step into. The power of impermanence is the thrill of the new.

1 | PP. 258–259
Bompas & Parr
for Idea Generation
Chewing Gum Factory, 2010

Photography: Simon Jacobs

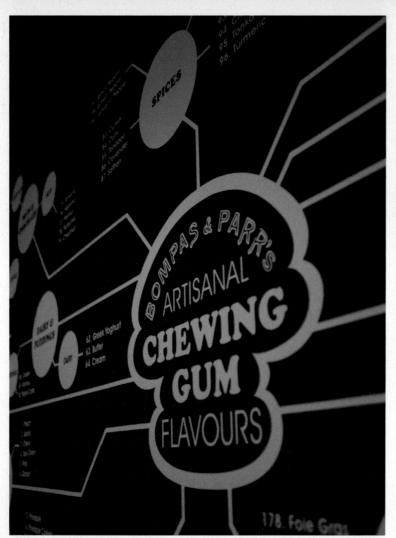

Commissioned by UK's largest arts and culture specialist PR agency Idea Generation, Bompas & Parr built an "artisanal" Chewing Gum Factory at Whiteleys Shopping Centre. Visitors learned the secrets of chewing gum manufacturing at the world's first gum microfactory. Each guest was able to choose and combine 200 familiar and unusual flavors, including iris, white truffle, tonic, curry, and beer yeast. In total, 40,000 flavor combinations were possible—including gums that changed flavor when chewed

Photography: Ann Charlott Ommedal

**Bompas & Parr
for Courvoisier**
Architectural Punchbowl, 2009

For the Architectural Punchbowl,

London, the Jelly company flooded 33 Portland Place with over four tons of punch—enough for 25,000 people. The punch bowl was so large that engineering firm Arup had to find a way to ensure

"With Courvoisier we flooded a grade one listed building with four tons of alcoholic punch that visitors boated across before drinking. There was enough to serve 25,000 people so it was pretty epic."

Bompas & Parr worked with the French cognac makers at Courvoisier to expand a cocktail to architectural scale. Resulting from a six-month research project with the University College of

that the building wouldn't collapse under the weight of all the alcohol. Visitors were able to across the punch before having a drink and toying with specially-designed remote controlled garnishes.

Photography: Barney Steel

**Bompas & Parr
for Truvia**
Voyage of Discovery, 2011

Bompas & Parr flooded part of the Selfridges Oxford Street branch roof to create a crystal island and boating lake in celebration of the impending UK arrival of Truvia calorie-free sweetener.

ing lake, thousands of stevia plants, 12 rowing boats, a gushing waterfall, a lifeguard, cocktails by ECC, design by Studio Toogood, uniforms by Tour de Force, tropical soundscapes by Dom James, teas by Rare Tea Company, coffees by Caravan, and a crystal island.

Photography: James Loveday [2], Beth Evans [3], Nathan Pask [4], Nick Westby [5]

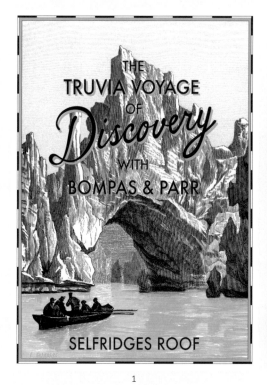

1

2

3

The Truvia Voyage of Discovery invited visitors to enjoy their first experience with the Truvia brand and their first introduction to its main ingredient, the stevia plant, astonishingly 200 times sweeter than sugar. The project encompassed an emerald green boat-

4

5

1

2

Portrait

1 2
Bompas & Parr
for Hendrick's
Alcoholic Architecture, 2009

3 4 5 6
Bompas & Parr
× Guerilla Science
for Wellcome Collection
Dirt Banquet, 2011

For Hendrick's Gin, Bompas & Parr opened a temporary bar in London's Soho district: Alcoholic Architecture, a walk-in cloud of breathable cocktail. Visitors were given protective suits before entering into a surreal scene filled with a mist of vaporized gin and tonic, which they imbibed through inhaling.

For the Wellcome collection, which is a London venue offering contemporary, historic, and natural science exhibitions, as well as collections, lively public events, and an extensive library for the incurably curious, Guerilla Science and Bompas & Parr hosted Dirt

"Every successful brand has a glorious story to tell. Sometimes it takes someone on the outside to tease it out."

Inspired by Antony Gormley's Blind Light installation at the Hayward Gallery and based on some professional advice by a company called JS Humidifiers, who produce industrial humidification systems, the jelly mongers used an ultrasonic humidifier to turn Hendrick's fine gin into a mist of the much-celebrated cocktail.

Photography: Dan Price[1], Greta Ilieva[2]

Banquet, a meal exploring the culinary implications of dirt. At Crossness Pumping Station, the Victorian cathedral to sewage, diners ate four courses and experienced a brown note, seated between four 52-ton pumps designed by Joseph Balgazette.

Photography: Ann Charlott Ommedal[3 4], Mike Massaro[5 6]

3

5

4

6

Wallpaper* × Æsir
Salon Dinners, 2011

Danish mobile phone maker Æsir and Wallpaper* magazine got together to co-host a series of intimate, experiential dinners featuring young Danish chef Bo Lindegaard, co-founder of the Copenhagen-based culinary venture "I'm a Kombo." Lindegaard's inventive specialties, created specifically for the dinners, were served in the modernist former home of the Commonwealth Institute, future home of the London Design Museum. This was only the first in a series of four extraordinary locations; after celebrating Wallpaper*'s Handmade Series and Æsir's contribution to the magazine's 2011 issue in London, the creative feast traveled to a beautiful decayed 1870s New York atrium building and a historic baroque palace in Moscow.

Photography: Jamie McGregor Smith, Ian Pierce

Formavision for Lexus
460 Degrees Gallery and Light and Speed Exhibition, 2007

For the launch of its new Sedan LS 460, luxury auto maker Lexus commissioned Formavision to create a temporary art installation that would travel to New York, Miami, Los Angeles, and Chicago. Taking the smooth and fluid driving experience of the new LS 460 as the starting point, Sebastien Agneessens and his team set up what they call the 460 Degrees Gallery. Home to the "Light and Speed Exhibition," the travelling gallery presented works by three international artists: Miranda Lichtenstein, Pascual Sisto, and Arne Quinze. Each artist's work interpreted the mental voyage of the car ride in different styles and media formats.

Photography: Dan Maddox

267

Formavision for Diesel
Diesel Denim Galleries, 2003 to 2007

Known for its eager involvement in the creative industries, Diesel entrusted Formavision with the development of a proper platform to showcase the brand's ambitious contributions to today's art scene. This resulted in the Diesel Denim Galleries, which combined the concept of the conventional retail space with that of an art gallery. Located in New York, Osaka, and Tokyo, Diesel Denim Galleries offered the best of Diesel's collection, while at the same time linking the brand to the contemporary art world. From 2003 to 2007, the galleries hosted a range of installations by various artists, who changed in a bimonthly rhythm—Korban/Flaubert's "Automatic," Jerszy Seymour's "Mo' Scum," and Jason Hackenwerth's "Dream of the Fisherman's Wife," to name only a few.

Photography: Jordan Kleinman

1

2

1
Formavision
× Korban Flaubert
Automatic

2
Formavision
× Jason Hackenwerth
Dream of the Fisherman's Wife

3

3
Formavision
× Jerszy Seymour

Mo' Scum

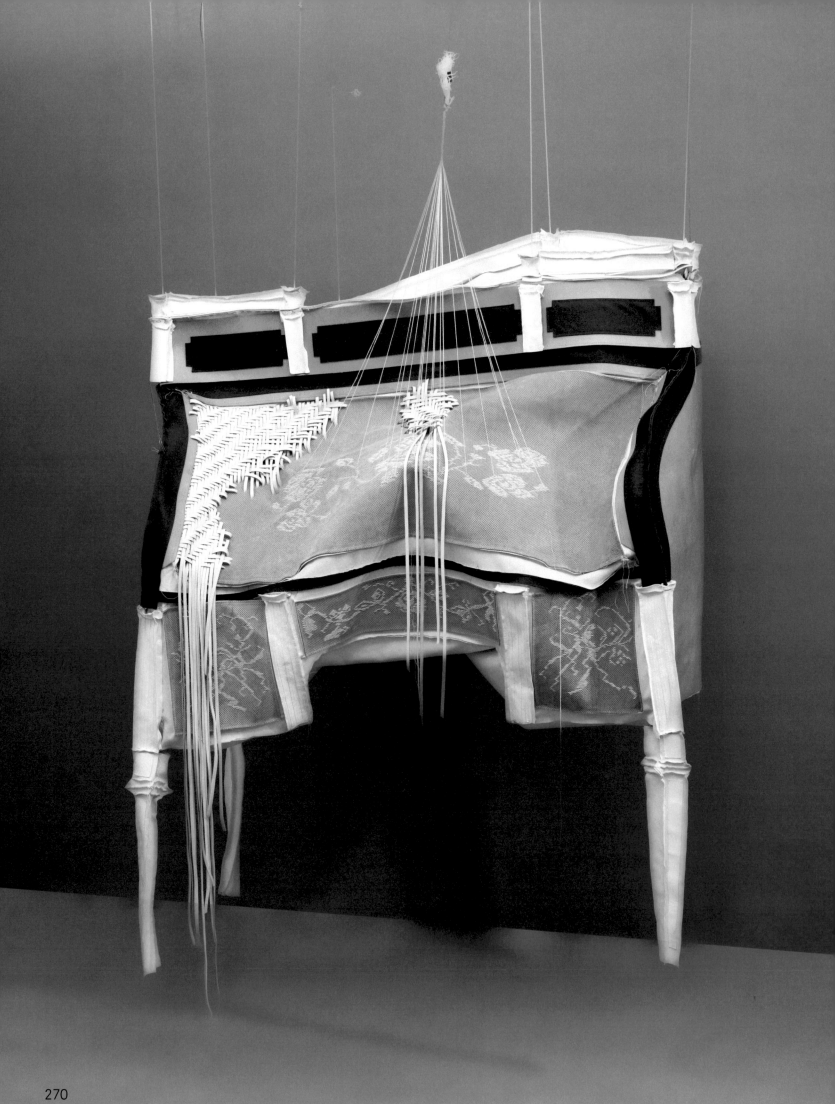

Fendi × Elisa Strozyk and Sebastian Neeb
Craft Alchemy, 2011

Fendi collaborated with designer Elisa Strozyk and artist Sebastian Neeb to create a joint 2011 Design Performance project at Design Miami. The result was an installation based on magical metamorphosis. Transforming discarded Fendi Selleria leather materials into fabulous pieces of furniture by means of embossing, sewing, braiding and woodworking, Elisa Strozyk and Sebastian Neeb celebrated Fendi's heritage by employing traditional craftwork materials. Their creations were set within an environment inspired by Palazzo Fendi, the grand Neoclassical building that houses Fendi's international headquarters, which was originally built around 1700 during the golden age of craftwork. Extending the Craft Alchemy theme into the design of Design Miami's exclusive Collectors Lounge, which Fendi hosted for the first time that year, Elisa Strozyk and Sebastian Neeb were invited to perform and demonstrate the processes of traditional craftwork that their creations are based on.

Fiona Leahy

PP.

272 – 279

Looking at her projects, one could imagine Fiona Leahy as a pixie with a glistening magic wand. Leahy agrees that she's constantly waving metaphorical wands, hoping to create magic.

Leahy founded her creative event, design, and productions agency in London in 2005. Having started her career as a fashion stylist for i-D magazine editor Patti Wilson and in iconic shoots with Terry Richardson, François Nars, and David LaChapelle, she went on to design fine jew-

work. I think that's perhaps what makes my work different: it's very informed by what is going on aesthetically in other worlds."

Poised between the classic and the contemporary, the theatrical polish of her creations blurs the line between reality and fiction. In an age of harsh brand competition and commercial practicality, Leahy's staged scenery celebrates beauty at its most decadent and it does so with ease and refreshing dreaminess. Countering the industry's realism with a certain fairy-land inventiveness, her

"Brands with history are fortunate as legacy is worth so much. However, even old brands need to change with the times and think of interesting was of capturing their customers' interest."

elry for the crown jewelers at Garrard and for Louis Vuitton. At Garrard, Leahy got increasingly involved with in-store events and parties, working alongside creative director Jade Jagger. At one of the Garrard events, she met Dita Von Teese, who asked Leahy to design and produce her wedding reception. Leahy says, "That was the catalyst. I haven't stopped in seven years."

Since then, a range of curious concepts have been realized under Leahy's creative direction. She has worked for clients such as Dasha Zhukova, Mark Ronson, Harvey Nichols, Christian Louboutin, and Middle Eastern royalty—often collaborating with teams of talented designers and coordinators to create occasions filled with enough bespoke elements, innovative detailing, and creative twists to stand out as proudly cherished specialties — even amidst the impressive abundance of the fashion industry.

Her fine grasp of the fashion scene and a keen sense of the extraordinary have been central to Leahy's recent rise to prominence. "I have a great appreciation for luxury and for beautiful things, and I love to channel that into my events. Art, fashion and style really do cross into my

projects turn consumption into unforgettable experience, visitors into honored guests and, eventually, into loyal brand ambassadors.

Entry to her shows is only granted to a select few and, as such, the very nature of Leahy's events signifies exclusivity. This may discourage direct affiliation. Instead, what is conveyed is the notion of a proudly-cherished peculiarity, shared with the masses only through multiplying stories on blogs and in the press—through occasional photographs of moments that have passed. Stories that evoke an aura of myth just beyond our immediate grasp are passed on, rather than documentary records. From a marketing perspective, this may have the calculated function of rumor, the purpose of which is to stimulate as much fantasy as possible.

Fiona Leahy knows and understands the sort of fantasy her clients aim to get across. "I think that because I have a fashion background that I can interpret brands' aesthetics more easily than if I had never worked in that world. I understand what fashion brands need to convey, but also I bring my own perspective to give it something unique and that transfers well into a memorable creative experience. Creativity, and also interpreting and respecting the creativity of others, is very important for me."

The starting point and foundation for her work is something that already exists: the brand's identity. What Leahy does is to strengthen it, and adapt it for different platforms and outlets. "So much of a brand's identity can be embraced— from logos to colors to mood to inspiration." Translating her client's identity into a language that reveals itself only to the senses, she presents the brand in its essence. The result is transient and yet immortal. These are unforgettable moments that turn the mundane into something sublime, that contradict the prevalent sense of mass-marketing irrelevance. The notion of myth becomes the art of the iconic.

1
Fiona Leahy Design
for Kova & T
Fashion Range Launch, 2007

For the launch of Dasha Zukhova's fashion range, Fiona Leahy and her team drew inspiration from the lace and latex within the Kova & T collection. Their "Urban Antointette" theme playfully mixed Marie Antoinette-style decadence with edgy modern aesthetics. FLD signature lace panels were

interwoven with the Kova & T Logo to incorporate the branding in a whimsical way. A gunmetal grey perspex table and a palette of grey and black urban tones was contrasted with feminine lace structures. Hand-crafted pastillage (sugar paste) place settings with each guest's name reflected the decadence of past centuries, as did towers of sweets and antique epergnes tumbling with vintage hued roses.

Fiona Leahy Design

"Brands come to us to inject a little magic and to visually manifest their creative identity."

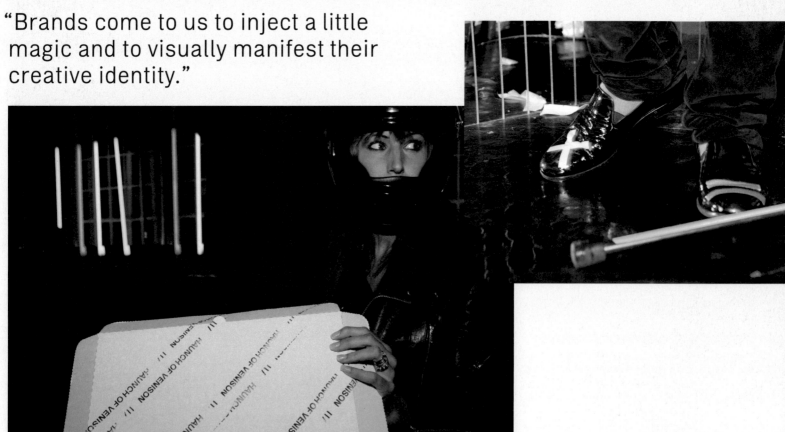

Fiona Leahy Design for Haunch of Venison
Rafael Lozano-Hemmer Launch, 2008

When Mexican artist Rafael Lozano-Hemmer's exhibition launched at London's Haunch of Venison Gallery during Frieze Art Fair 2008, Fiona Leahy Design threw the party. Drawing on the artist's involvement with electronic and often light-related material, the designers created fluorescent scenenery for the celebration.

The party featured mirror installations, giant tie-dyed paper fruit, and rows of neon tubes, transforming the Bloomsbury Ballroom into neon Mexicana. Leather-clad models masquerading as motorcycle couriers served Haunch of Venison pizza & tiki tequila cocktails, while guests danced to Dan Lywood & Sneaky Sound System's infectious live set.

"Impermanence is part of the magic—going from nothing to something incredible that then disappears."

Fiona Leahy Design

Fiona Leahy Design
for ELLE UK
ELLE Style Awards, 2010

Fiona Leahy and her team are fascinated with paper artistry, and figured that an event for a print magazine posed a good opportunity to elaborate on the fragile and yet so utilitarian material. For ELLE and its Style Awards at the Grand Connaught Rooms in London, they made use of the physicality of the fashion publication itself, recycling its printed pages to become the stuff of beautiful forms at this glorious event.

"Spending time alone is very important for me when dreaming up magical scenarios. I am inspired by art exhibitions, fashion shows and craft. I also find inspiration in the most random of places— antique shops, car boot sales, fairgrounds...the list goes on."

Fiona Leahy Design

Fiona Leahy Design
for Stella McCartney
Stella McCartney Eco Line Launch, 2009

To celebrate the launch of her first eco-clothing line, Stella McCartney invited her guests to gather in her Fiona Leahy-designed wonderland at the Harvey Nichols London store. On arriv-

al, giant pink flower-embellished letters spelled out the designer's name in floral topiaries, and graffiti branding lined the walls. Posies of dusty pink peonies and personalized friendship bracelets marked each place setting under a chandelier-like arrangement of multitudinous lanterns.

Artist/Designer Index

F – M

Artist/Designer Index

T – X

Company Index

A – D

Company Index

R – Z

Taken By Surprise

Cutting-Edge Collaborations between
Designers, Artists and Brands

Edited by Robert Klanten, Sven Ehmann,
and Anna Sinofzik
Text and preface by Anna Sinofzik

Cover by Floyd E. Schulze for Gestalten
Cover images:
Nendo Photography by Daici Ano
Erwin Wurm Studio Wurm;
Courtesy of Gallery Thaddaeus Ropac
Sarah Illenberger Photography by
Ragnar Schmuck
Gerry Judah Photography by David Barbour

Layout by Floyd E. Schulze for Gestalten
Typeface: Zimmer by Julian Hansen
Foundry: www.gestaltenfonts.com

Project management by
Rebekka Wangler for Gestalten
Project management assistance by
Andres Ramirez for Gestalten
Production management by
Martin Bretschneider for Gestalten
Proofreading by Elvia Wilk
Printed by Eberl Print, Immenstadt im Allgäu
Made in Germany

Published by Gestalten, Berlin 2012
ISBN 978-3-89955-421-2

For more information, please visit
www.gestalten.com.

Bibliographic information published by
the Deutsche Nationalbibliothek.
The Deutsche Nationalbibliothek
lists this publication in the Deutsche
Nationalbibliografie; detailed bibliographic data are available online at
http://dnb.d-nb.de.

None of the content in this book was
published in exchange for payment
by commercial parties or designers;
Gestalten selected all included work
based solely on its artistic merit.

This book was printed according to the
internationally accepted ISO 14001
standards for environmental protection,
which specify requirements for an environmental management system.

This book was printed on paper certified
by the FSC®.

FSC
www.fsc.org
MIX
Paper from
responsible sources
FSC® C002727

Gestalten is a climate-neutral company. We collaborate with the non-
profit carbon offset provider myclimate
(www.myclimate.org) to neutralize the
company's carbon footprint produced
through our worldwide business activities by investing in projects that reduce
CO_2 emissions (www.gestalten.com/
myclimate).

myclimate
Protect our planet

420213